Who
Decides ?

*Making Decisions on Behalf
of Mentally Incapacitated Adults*

*A CONSULTATION PAPER ISSUED BY
THE LORD CHANCELLOR'S DEPARTMENT*

*Presented to Parliament by the Lord High Chancellor
by Command of Her Majesty*

December 1997

Cm 3803   £12.70

How to Respond to the Green Paper

This Consultation Paper is circulated for comment. It does not represent the settled views of the Government. In some areas, the Government has indicated its preliminary views in the paper which will be reviewed in the light of comments received.

The Lord Chancellor's Department would be grateful to receive comments on the paper by **31 March 1998**. Responses received after that date will not be taken into account.

Responses should be addressed to:

Chris Miles
Family Policy Division
Lord Chancellor's Department
Room 5.14
Selborne House
54 – 60 Victoria Street
London
SW1E 6QW

Tel: 0171 210 8871

Responses can also be e-mailed to the following address:
enquiries.lcdhq@gtnet.gov.uk

It would be particularly helpful if responses could be set out in the order of the questions in the Paper. A summary of consultation questions is given in Annex A of the Paper.

Any request to treat all, or part, of a reply in confidence will of course be respected. If no such request is made it will be assumed that the reply is not intended to be confidential.

Contents

Contents

4 ***Advance Statements about Health Care*** **23**

This Chapter looks at one of the more sensitive areas of the Law Commission's work: their recommendations on advance statements (which are also commonly referred to as advance directives, living wills, or, where the statement refuses treatment, advance refusals). The Chapter observes that advance refusals already have full effect at common law, but seeks views on whether the Government should be legislating in this area, and if so, what should be the aim of such legislation. The Law Commission's recommendations are examined closely as a possible model for legislation, should respondents think legislation is appropriate.

5 ***Independent Supervision of Medical and Research Procedures*** **33**

This Chapter considers another area of particular sensitivity: the supervision of medical and research procedures, including sterilisation, donation of tissue or bone marrow, and abortion. The Law Commission recommended independent supervision to ensure that the best interests of the person without capacity are protected in all circumstances. The Government wishes to ensure that there are sufficient safeguards.

6 ***Continuing Powers of Attorney*** **43**

The Law Commission recommended a significant extension of the existing system of powers of attorney and Enduring Powers of Attorney. Their final Report suggested an unified scheme to provide for substitute decision-making procedures. A Continuing Power of Attorney is recommended, which would allow an attorney to make decisions relating to personal welfare, health care and financial matters, even after the donor of the power of attorney has lost capacity. The Green Paper seeks views on the scope and nature of the proposed scheme, and on the appropriate safeguards.

7   *Decision-Making by the Court*   **55**

This Chapter considers the Law Commission's recommendations for a single integrated judicial framework for the making of decisions relating to personal welfare, healthcare and financial matters. The Law Commission recommended that the court should be able to make one-off orders where necessary, or appoint a manager with continuing powers. Although not covered in the Law Commission's Report, this Chapter also seeks views on whether, and how, managers of residential care and nursing homes should be allowed to manage the funds of residents without capacity.

8   *Public Law Protection for People at Risk*   **67**

This Chapter considers whether there is a need for reform of emergency powers for public officials to be able to intervene in the lives of persons with certain types of disability, including the power to arrange that they be removed from their homes. It should be noted that the Law Commission's definition of vulnerable adults in this area is wider than the definition of those without capacity which applies to other areas of their final Report. This Chapter reflects that more widely defined client group. The Government seeks views on the Law Commission's recommendations, and wishes to ensure that, if the law in this area is to be reformed, there is an appropriate balance between protecting vulnerable adults, and respect for individual rights.

Contents

9 *Judicial Forum*   *75*

In order to enable the various judicial decisions required within other sections of the Report to be made, the Law Commission recommended a new role for the Court of Protection, and the Public Trust Office. This Chapter examines those recommendations.

Introduction

1.1.   The Government believes there is a clear need for reform of the law in order to improve and clarify the decision-making process for those who are unable to make decisions for themselves, or those who cannot communicate their decisions. These are some of the most vulnerable people in our society. The law in this area has developed in piecemeal fashion, and does not always offer sufficient protection either for mentally incapacitated adults, or for those who look after them.

1.2.   This Consultation Paper seeks views on a possible framework for providing that protection, and for providing an organised framework of law to manage the welfare and affairs of mentally incapacitated adults.

THE WORK OF THE LAW COMMISSION

1.3.   The Government's consideration of this area is based on the work of the Law Commission, and this Consultation Paper follows closely the recommendations included in their report *Mental Incapacity*[1]. That report, which offers a coherent and broad scheme for the reform of the law in this area, was the culmination of five years work and four other Consultation Papers:

Mentally Incapacitated Adults and Decision-Making – An Overview[2]

Mentally Incapacitated Adults and Decision-Making: A New Jurisdiction[3]

Mentally Incapacitated Adults and Decision-Making: Medical Treatment and Research[4]

Mentally Incapacitated and Other Vulnerable Adults: Public Law Protection[5]

THE GOVERNMENT'S APPROACH

1.4.   The Government sees considerable merit in the work of the Law Commission on these issues, and in a number of areas the Government is minded to accept the principles underlying the Law Commission's recommendations. Those areas include the report's proposals on:

---

1   *Law Com 231, published in February 1995.*

2   *Consultation Paper No 119, published in April 1991.*

3   *Consultation Paper No 128, published in February 1993.*

4   *Consultation Paper No 129, published in April 1993.*

5   *Consultation Paper No 130, published in May 1993.*

the definition of incapacity;

a framework for carers which would remove the present uncertainty;

more extensive powers for the Court of Protection so that decisions can be made regarding a person's health care, personal welfare and finance within the same jurisdiction; and

powers of attorney for the care of the person.

1.5. Consultation in these areas is aimed at ensuring that the detailed recommendations made by the Law Commission are considered appropriate and practical. On a number of issues, the Government wishes to ensure there are sufficient safeguards in place for the protection not only of patients, but also those charged with their care.

1.6. There are areas of the Law Commission's final report which raise issues of particular moral and ethical sensitivity, and on which the Government recognises that people hold strong personal views. These areas include:

advance statements about health care; and

non-therapeutic research;

1.7. The Government recognises that advance refusals of treatment are currently binding at common law and supports the patient's right to decide whether to accept treatment and to make an advance directive expressing their refusal of a course of action or a particular treatment. Bearing in mind the strong personal views held on these subjects, the Government believes further full public consultation is necessary before considering whether to put this on a statutory footing to ensure that those views can be fully expressed. The sections of this Green Paper which deal with these issues ask general questions about whether or not the Government should legislate in this area, and, if so, what should be the objectives of that legislation. In each case, in addition to these broad questions, the Government seeks detailed views on the Law Commission's proposals. This should not be taken as prejudicial to the outcome of consultation on the broader questions about whether these are areas that should be taken forward. Rather, the Government wants to ensure that, if these areas are considered appropriate for legislation, the proposals for that legislation have had the benefit of full public scrutiny.

Euthanasia

1.8. There is a widespread misconception which links advance statements and euthanasia. The law currently makes a clear distinction between advance statements, which are lawful, and which allow a patient to indicate in advance of any subsequent incapacity the sort of treatment he or she would, or would not, consent to, and euthanasia, which is a deliberate intervention with the express aim of ending life. Euthanasia is illegal. An advance statement cannot direct a doctor to do anything which is illegal. The Government has no plans to change the law in this respect. The Government therefore shares the view of the House of Lords Select Committee on Medical Ethics[6] **that there should be no move toward the legalisation of euthanasia.** The Law Commission made no recommendations on euthanasia in their report on mental incapacity, and this Consultation Paper will not be seeking views on this subject.

---

6 *See paragraphs 2.17-2.18, below*

RESOURCES

1.9. There can be little doubt that, if a scheme of the type proposed by the Law Commission were implemented, there would be additional resources required, and additional cost. In particular, there would be additional operational costs for the Public Trust Office and the Court of Protection, the Official Solicitor, the National Health Service, social services departments, and the magistrates' courts, with financial costs also to the legal aid fund. In line with the Government's determination to contain public spending, and not to increase the tax burden, it would be necessary to recover a substantial contribution to added costs from actual or potential beneficiaries of the new procedures. The Government would therefore welcome views on the likely resource implications, and their affordability, weighed against the merit of what must be issues of singular moral and ethical importance.

Q1a. **What resource implications do those working in this area envisage would result for them and for other parties from the proposals?**

Q1b. **Would the likely benefits render the costs incurred worthwhile?**

Q1c. **How should these costs be met?**

SCOPE OF CONSULTATION

1.10. This Paper considers the scope for reform of the law for managing the affairs of those unable to make decisions for themselves in England and Wales. The Paper does not relate to Northern Ireland, nor Scotland.

Developments in Scotland

1.11. The Scottish Law Commission has also considered the law in this area, and it published its report on Incapable Adults in September 1995[7]. The previous Government issued a Consultation Paper[8] in February 1997. Comments were requested by the end of April and over 160 were received.

1.12. Although the underlying principles of the Scottish Law Commission's approach are broadly similar to the stance taken in England and Wales, there are some differences. For example, in Scotland it is proposed that there is to be a certification process for powers of attorney intended to continue on the incapacity of the donor, that requires a solicitor to confirm that the donor understands the arrangement and is not acting under duress. The proposals for intromissions with an incapable adult's bank account are different in Scotland, as is the proposal that managers of residential establishments may be authorised to manage funds of their incapable residents up to a prescribed limit.

1.13. The Government is considering its policy for Scotland in the light of the responses to the consultation exercise. The medical aspects of the two Law Commissions' reports are sufficiently similar that careful consideration will be required of taking a common GB-wide approach in this area. Given the different existing framework of statutory and common law in Scotland, other provisions can be expected to vary, even though the underlying principles are shared.

---

7   *Scot Law Com No 151.*

8   *Managing the Finances and Welfare of Incapable Adults, The Stationery Office, February 1997.*

Q2. *Should a common GB-wide approach be given to the health matters covered by the Law Commission and Scottish Law Commission?*

Application to adults only

1.14. The Law Commission considered whether their proposals should apply only to those aged 18 or over, or whether they should include those aged 16 and 17. Respondents to their consultation exercise indicated that it is common for those aged 16 and 17 to be included in arrangements made for adults, rather than arrangements made for younger children. It was also noted that it would be wasteful to have to initiate two separate sets of legal proceedings for those who are close to the age of majority. There was general support, therefore, for the proposals contained within the Law Commission's Report applying to those aged 16 or over. Some of the proposals do, however, apply only to those aged 18 or over, and these are identified in this Paper. The Government is minded to accept this recommendation, subject to the views of consultees.

Q3. *Should the provisions recommended by the Law Commission apply only to those aged 16 or over?*

Inter-relationship with the criminal law

1.15. This Paper does not analyse in detail the interrelationship between the Law Commission's recommended statutory decision-making processes on behalf of mentally incapacitated adults, and the criminal law. Once responses to the Green Paper have been considered and the issues have been taken further forward, detailed consideration will be given to the interrelationship with the criminal law. The Government's conclusions will be set out as part of a more general policy statement at that stage. There will, of course, be no proposals to change the law relating to euthanasia.

STRUCTURE OF THE PAPER

1.16. This Green Paper has been written so as to be free-standing, although it has been structured to follow the Law Commission's Report *Mental Incapacity*. Respondents may wish to refer to the Law Commission's Report for a fuller analysis of their recommendations. (The Report is available from HMSO, ISBN 0-10-218995-1.) The Law Commission's Report contains a comprehensive analysis of the current law in this area. This Paper does not provide a further analysis of the current law.

1.17. The remainder of this Paper is therefore organised as follows. A background chapter (chapter 2) precedes discussion on the three key principles underlying work in this area: the definitions of "capacity", "best interests" and the "general authority to act reasonably" (chapter 3). Chapters 4 and 5 consider the issues of advance statements and the independent supervision of medical and research procedures. Chapter 6 looks at the recommendations on a Continuing Powers of Attorney (CPA) scheme. Chapter 7 considers the proposals for a unified system of judicial decision-making to cover financial, personal welfare and health care matters. Chapter 8 seeks views on the proposed provision of public law protection for people at risk (not just those who suffer from a mental incapacity). Chapter 9 considers the proposals for a new judicial forum.

Background

2.1. A wide range of conditions can result in incapacity to take decisions. In some cases, the capacity to take decisions is never attained (for example in the case of some people with a learning disability). In other cases, capacity is attained but is subsequently lost. This may occur for a number of reasons, including medical disorders and traumatic injury. The loss of capacity may be temporary for example during a toxic confusional state, which might result from an illness, or the use of drugs. In some cases, capacity may fluctuate; an example would be manic-depressive disorder where the person may have full capacity during periods when they are well, but may lose it during periods of illness. Finally, the loss of capacity may be permanent, as for example in some cases of dementia or the persistent vegetative state (PVS). Many of the proposals made by the Law Commission are primarily relevant to all those who are incapacitated, but the recommendations concerning serious medical procedures are likely to be primarily relevant to those whose period of incapacity is expected to be either prolonged or permanent. In responding to the questions raised in the Paper the different circumstances which may have resulted in incapacity should be borne in mind.

THE CHANGING FACE OF HEALTH CARE AND SERVICES FOR THOSE WITHOUT CAPACITY
The population
2.2. The number of people over 85 will increase by over 30% in this decade. Advances in health care and in living standards mean that many people will now live longer. The incidence of incapacity increases as people get older. Dementia of all types affects over 5% of all those over the age of 65. In those over 80, the figure rises to 20%. The changes in population structure have consequently made the issue of decision making for those who become incapacitated increasingly important.

MEDICAL ADVANCES
2.3. Advances in health care mean not only that people are likely to live longer, but also in circumstances and with illnesses and disabilities which previously would have led to the person's death.

2.4. Palliative care is a special type of care for people whose illness may no longer be curable. It focuses on controlling pain and other distressing symptoms as well as providing emotional and spiritual support. It enables patients to achieve the best possible quality of life during the final stages of their illness. The Government is committed to the provision of palliative care and money to provide this service is now built into health authority general allocations. Health authorities contract with their local providers, usually in the voluntary sector, for the services they require, based on the assessed health needs of their resident population.

2.5. A patient cannot demand a particular form of treatment – that is a matter for the clinical judgement of the doctor. He or she can, however, refuse. The Government fully supports the right of a patient to receive sufficient information about a proposed treatment to enable him or her to make a decision about whether or not to consent to it being carried out.

2.6. The Government has always emphasised that it does not accept that the individual's right to determine the treatment he or she is prepared to refuse or accept extends to any action deliberately taken to end the patient's life. The Government fully supports the view of the House of Lords Select Committee on Medical Ethics that euthanasia is unacceptable and should remain an offence of murder.

THE COURT OF PROTECTION AND THE PUBLIC TRUST OFFICE[1]

2.7. The Court of Protection exists to safeguard the interests of anyone who is 'incapable by reason of mental disorder of managing and administering his property and affairs'. Anyone found on medical evidence to meet these criteria is known as 'a patient'. The Court's duties are normally carried out by appointing a receiver for a patient. The receiver acts as a statutory agent whose powers are limited and specified in the order appointing him and in any further directions or authorities issued by the Court or the Public Trust Office. The Mental Health Act 1983 gives the Court power to authorise virtually any transaction on behalf of a patient and to do whatever is necessary or expedient for the maintenance or benefit of the patient, his family and dependants. The Court's administrative functions are now carried out by the Public Trust Office[2].

2.8. An alternative way of administering the financial affairs of mentally incapacitated people was provided by the Enduring Powers of Attorney Act 1985. This Act made it possible for certain powers of attorney granted in a special form to endure beyond the period of capacity.[3] Such agreements must be registered with the Court of Protection when the attorney has reason to believe that the donor is or is becoming mentally incapable. By the end of 1996, nearly 34,000 of

---

1 *Annex D contains further information about the Court of Protection, the Public Trust Office and the Official Solicitor.*

2 *The relationship between the Public Trust Office and the Court of Protection evolved during the 1980s and is often imperfectly understood. This sometimes causes confusion about the respective roles of the two bodies. In 1986, the bureaucracy of the Court was dismantled with the large majority of its staff being transferred to the Public Trust Office. The Court itself became a purely judicial body consisting of the Master and two Assistant Masters with a small support staff, exercising the limited judicial functions now defined in rule 6 of the Court of Protection Rules 1994 and powers under the Enduring Powers of Attorney Act 1985. At any one time, the number of cases handled by the Court (which has 10 staff compared to the Public Trust Office's 580) is very small.*

3 *Under the existing law, a person (the donor) with capacity can give an ordinary power of attorney to another person (the attorney) which gives the donee authority to act on the donor's behalf in relation to the donor's property. The power of attorney can be general and relate to all the donor's property or specific and, for example, give the donee authority to act only in relation to one property. The donor of the power cannot give the donee power to do anything in relation to the property which he himself could not do. The main disadvantage of ordinary powers of attorney for the purpose of managing the affairs of vulnerable people is that they terminate on incapacity.*

these agreements had been registered at the Court of Protection. Many others will have been prepared but not registered.

THE OFFICIAL SOLICITOR

2.9.   A central element of the Official Solicitor's duties is safeguarding the welfare, property and status of persons under a legal disability or at a disadvantage before the law. He deals with some 950 new cases of proceedings involving adults under mental incapacity each year. Many of these relate to a wide spread of litigation of all categories, mainly affecting financial rights or liabilities, from possession actions in the county courts to heavy personal injuries litigation in the High Court, but two increasingly important areas of work are declaratory proceedings in the High Court and medical treatment decisions. The former include cases where the issues centre on where a person under disability is to live and with whom he or she is to have contact. The latter require him to act as guardian ad litem or amicus curiae in respect of treatment such as sterilisation, abortion, emergency caesareans and end-of-life decisions such as the withdrawal of nutrition and hydration from a patient in a persistent vegetative state.

2.10.   The judiciary and staff of the Court of Protection, the Public Trust Office and the Official Solicitor's Office have built up a great expertise in assisting those who have limited or no capacity to make decisions for themselves. Although, strictly speaking, the current jurisdiction is limited to financial matters, this can be a hard dividing line to draw in practice.

SOCIAL SECURITY APPOINTEES

2.11.   Under existing legislation, the Secretary of State for Social Security may appoint a person over 18 years of age to act on behalf of a claimant who, because of a mental incapacity, is unable to manage his or her own affairs. As well as individuals, the appointee can be an organisation such as a local authority or a health authority.

2.12.   Appointee action is normally instigated by an application from the prospective appointee. An officer from the Benefits Agency will then interview the incapacitated person to confirm that they are unable to manage their own affairs. If there is any doubt about the person's capabilities, medical evidence should be obtained. The officer will also interview the applicant to explain the responsibilities of an appointee and confirm that they are suitable to act.

2.13.   Once a person has been appointed to act the appointment is open-ended. At present, the Department of Social Security does not routinely monitor appointee arrangements. However, the Secretary of State can revoke an appointeeship at any time if it is brought to her attention that the appointee is not complying with the conditions on which it was granted.

2.14.   Although the Law Commission made no firm recommendations relating to Social Security Appointees, and the subject is not considered in detail as part of this consultation exercise, the Department of Social Security would be interested in receiving any feedback on how well the current arrangements work, and how the system could be improved.

THE EUROPEAN CONVENTION ON HUMAN RIGHTS

2.15. The Government has considered whether or not the Law Commission's recommendations are likely to comply with the European Convention on Human Rights. The policy aims for the Commission's project on decision-making on behalf of mentally incapacitated adults were:

> that people are enabled and encouraged to take for themselves those decisions which they are able to take;

> that where it is necessary in their own interests or for the protection of others that someone else should take those decisions on their behalf, the intervention should be as limited as possible and should be concerned to achieve what the person himself would have wanted; and

> that the proper safeguards should be provided against exploitation and neglect, and against physical, sexual or psychological abuse.

2.16. The Government cannot predict the nature and outcome of all types of claims of violation of the Convention which may arise if the Law Commission's recommendations are enacted. Nevertheless, the Government considers that by adopting a new decision-making process for those who do not have capacity to make the decision, which pays particular regard to the person without capacity's right to self determination (where possible), the person's human rights should be protected. However, the Government would like to know of any concerns which respondents may have regarding the Law Commission's proposals in so far as the ECHR is concerned.

> **Q4.   Do respondents have any concerns regarding the Law Commission's recommendations in so far as the ECHR is concerned?**

OTHER PROJECTS
House of Lords Select Committee on Medical Ethics

2.17. The Government has also been greatly assisted by the report of the House of Lords Select Committee on Medical Ethics. The Select Committee was appointed, under the chairmanship of Lord Walton of Detchant, to consider the ethical, legal and clinical implications of a person's right to withhold consent to life-giving treatment, and the position of persons who are no longer able to give or withhold consent; and to consider whether and in what circumstances actions that have as their intention or a likely consequence the shortening of another person's life may be justified on the grounds that they accord with that person's wishes or with that person's best interests; and in the light of all the foregoing considerations to pay regard to the likely effects of changes in law or medical practice on society as a whole.

2.18. The Select Committee reported to Parliament in February 1994[4] and the report was debated in the House of Lords in May 1994[5]. The report overlaps with, and in many areas complements, the work of the Law Commission. The Government has drawn on evidence submitted to the Select Committee in preparing this Consultation Paper.

---

4   *Report of the Select Committee on Medical Ethics (1993-94) HL 21-I*

5   *Hansard (HL) 9 May 1994, vol. 554, col. 1344.*

British Medical Association (BMA) Code of Practice

2.19. In response to a recommendation from the House of Lords Select Committee on Medical Ethics, the British Medical Association set up a working group with representatives of other health professionals to produce a Code of Practice on Advance Statements for health professionals. This was published on 5 April 1995. The BMA also collaborated with the Patients Association to produce a guide for patients concerning advance statements, which was published in 1996.

Council of Europe Convention on Human Rights and Biomedicine

2.20. The Council of Europe Convention on Human Rights and Biomedicine was opened for signature in April 1997. The Convention gives a central place to the principle of consent and the importance of protecting those without capacity to consent. The Convention provides that with strict safeguards, patients not able to consent may donate regenerative tissue such as bone marrow and participate in research. The Convention only has legal force if ratified by a Member State, and it permits Member States to set higher standards of protection than required by the Convention if they wish.

2.21. The Convention contains a wide range of complex ethical and legal issues which the Government is considering carefully before reaching a decision on signature or ratification.

Hague Convention

2.22. The Hague Conference on Private International Law is in the process of negotiating a draft Convention on the protection of adults. This does not deal with matters of substantive law, but with arrangements between Contracting States for determining jurisdiction, and with administrative and co-operative arrangements for dealing with matters that arise in relation to the protection of adults. The text of a preliminary draft Convention was agreed in September 1997, and this will be the subject of further negotiation. The Convention which results will only have legal force if ratified by a Member State.

Consultation on the removal, storage and use of gametes

2.23. In September this year, the Government issued a separate Consultation Paper concerning the removal, storage and use of gametes without consent. These matters will therefore not be taken forward separately as part of the consideration of this Green Paper. Those wishing to address these issues should contact Michael Evans at the Department of Health (Room 423, Wellington House, 133-155 Waterloo Road, London SE1 8UG). It should be noted, however, that responses to that consultation exercise are requested by *31 December 1997*.

Offences Against the Person Act 1861

2.24. The Government will shortly be consulting on its proposals to reform the Offences Against the Person Act 1861 based upon the recommendations of the Law Commission in "Offences Against the Person and General Principles"[6]. This consultation paper will seek views on some of the difficult issues around the technical legal changes proposed by the Law Commission and will include a draft Bill.

6   *Law Com 218*

The Key Principles

Capacity, Best Interests, and the General Authority to Act Reasonably

BACKGROUND

3.1. This chapter focuses on the concepts of capacity, best interests and the general authority to act reasonably, which underpin the Law Commission's proposals. The Law Commission's suggested definitions for these concepts received broad support on consultation.

3.2. The Government supports the principles behind the Law Commission's proposals in this area, but seeks views in this chapter, on whether the proposed definitions are practical and workable.

THE TEST OF CAPACITY

3.3. The Law Commission recommended a new statutory definition of incapacity[1].

Presumption against lack of capacity

3.4. The Law Commission recommended that there be a presumption against lack of capacity. This conforms with current principles of common law. It also supports the general principle that there should be minimal intervention in the affairs of individuals unless there is a demonstrable need to do so. This is a common sense approach, and the Government notes the wide support the Law Commission received for this on consultation.

3.5. The Government accepts this recommendation in principle.

Determining whether an individual lacks capacity

3.6. The Law Commission considered a number of possible approaches to the definition of capacity, but favoured the "functional approach", which is currently the main method used in common law. This received overwhelming support on consultation.

3.7. This approach focuses on the decision itself and the capability of the person concerned to understand at the time it is made the nature of the decision required and its implications. This approach is thus very specific and avoids generalisations which may involve unnecessary intrusion into the affairs of the individual. For example, a person may be able to decide that they want to have contact with a particular relative, but may not be able to understand the nature of a particular financial contract on which a decision is needed. The functional approach would

---

1 *Law Com 231, para. 3.23.*

indicate that the first decision is one for which the person had capacity, whereas the second decision is one for which s/he did not. The approach thus allows individuals to have the maximum decision-making powers possible. Restrictions would be dependent on the nature and complexity of the decision in hand and would not exclude the person from making decisions within their competence.

3.8.   The Government accepts this recommendation.

A diagnostic threshold

3.9.   The Law Commission consulted on the possibility of linking the test of capacity and the concept of "mental disorder" as defined in the Mental Health Act 1983. This possibility was rejected, the Law Commission considering that:

> this was insufficiently broad to be able to deal with all possible scenarios; and

> there would be few, outside those specialising in mental health, who understood exactly what this meant.

3.10.   The Law Commission thus recommended that the expression "mental disability"[2] be used (except in cases where the person is unable to communicate) and should mean 'any disability or disorder of the mind or brain, whether permanent or temporary, which results in an impairment or disturbance of mental functioning'[3].

3.11.   The Law Commission recommended that the test of incapacity should also apply to the communication of a decision as well as the ability to make the decision itself. This would cover cases where it is not possible to determine the person's response, even if they might be capable of making the decision concerned. They thus suggested that a person should be regarded as without capacity if at the material time (the time of the decision) he or she is:

> "– unable by reason of mental disability to make a decision on the matter in question; or

> – unable to communicate a decision on that matter because he or she is unconscious or for any other reason."[4]

3.12.   The Government accepts this recommendation in principle, but seeks views on whether these definitions are considered appropriate.

Further definition of inability to make a decision

3.13.   The Law Commission suggested that the inability to make a decision could be split into two areas: the first question is whether the person concerned is able to understand and retain the relevant information, including the consequences, not only of deciding one way or another but also of making no decision at all. The second question is whether the disability means that the

---

2   *In reaching the conclusion that there should be a diagnostic threshold the Law Commission took into account that there may be a small number of cases where a finding of incapacity could lead to action which could amount to 'detention' within the meaning of Article 5 of the European Convention on Human Rights. The case law of the European Court of Human Rights requires that any such detention should be pursuant to a finding of unsoundness of mind based on "objective medical expertise" (see para 3.8 of the Commission's Report and Consultation Paper No 119, paras 3.10 – 3.14).*

3   *Law Com 231, para. 3.12.*

4   *Ibid., para. 3.14.*

person concerned is able to use that information in order to arrive at a decision: some people may be unable to exert their will, whether because of delusions or compulsions, or because of susceptibility to influence, or any other reason connected with their disability. The schizophrenic who cannot believe what his doctors or financial advisors tell him is one example; the manic depressive whose impulses override his understanding is another. This is supported by Thorpe J's judgement in *Re C*[5]. The Law Commission thus recommended that a person should be regarded as unable to make a decision by reason of mental disability if the disability is such that, at the time when the decision needs to be made, the person is:

> unable to understand or retain the information relevant to the decision or

> unable to make a decision based on that information.

3.14. The recommendations made by the Law Commission in this area were generally well supported on consultation and they reflect the type of issues taken into account in common law at present.

3.15. The case of *Re MB*[6] has further clarified the common law in this area. In this case, the Court of Appeal set out the principles determining whether a person lacks capacity. The court also set out principles of procedure to be followed when it is thought necessary to seek declarations from the courts on such a matter. In the light of this, and a number of similar cases, the Department of Health has already issued a summary of legal rulings to the NHS, under cover of an Executive Letter[7], concerning the legal rulings in relation to caesarean sections and to the posthumous storage of gametes.

Q5a. Is the proposed definition of incapacity appropriate, and likely to be of use to practitioners?

Q5b. If so, how do practitioners see this working in practice?

Code of Practice

3.16. The Law Commission suggested a Code of Practice for the guidance of those assessing whether a person is or is not without capacity to make decisions. As well as providing valuable guidance for professionals, such a Code of Practice might also help deal with a number of practical problems, such as that of the individual whose mental state varies widely and who fluctuates between capacity and incapacity.

3.17. The Government accepts the principle of this recommendation.

Maximising decision-making capacity

3.18. To maximise the person's potential to make their own decisions, the Law Commission recommended that a person should not be regarded as unable to understand the information relevant to a decision if he or she is able to understand an explanation of that information in broad terms and simple language, including other languages if appropriate or other forms of communication such as audio tapes. They also recommended that a person should not be regarded as incapable of communicating their decisions unless "all practicable steps to enable him or her to do so have been taken without success"[8].

---

5 *Re C (Adult: Refusal of treatment)[1994] 1 WLR 290.*

6 *Re MB (Medical Treatment) [1997] 2FLR No3.*

7 *EL(97)32 Consent to Treatment – Summary of Legal Rulings*

8 *Law Com 231, para. 3.21*

3.19. The Government accepts the principle of this recommendation, but seeks views on how these proposals would work in practice.

> **Q6.** *How, in practice, should "all practicable steps" be defined?*

> **Q7.** *When would it be reasonable to conclude that such steps had been taken?*

3.20. The Law Commission's final recommendation in this area concerns the resulting decision, which they maintained should not be regarded as invalid, just because it would "not be made by a person with ordinary prudence". This again asserts the right of the individual to make their own choices, even if these do not comply with those of professional experts, or are made for reasons which are irrational, unknown or for no reason at all.

3.21. The Government accepts the principle of this recommendation, but seeks respondents' views on how best consistency can be ensured in determining whether a person is unable to make a decision, and whether the Law Commission's proposals offer sufficient guidance for practitioners.

> **Q8.** *How best can consistency be ensured in the determining of inability to make a decision?*

> **Q9.** *Do the Law Commission's definitions of inability to make a decision offer sufficient guidance for medical practitioners?*

BEST INTERESTS

3.22. There is little doubt that decisions made on behalf of a person without capacity should be made in their best interests. Respondents to the Law Commission's consultation were almost unanimous in their acceptance of this point, and the Government shares this view, subject to the confirmation of respondents that the approach is appropriate.

> **Q10.** *Is the best interests approach the most appropriate for making decisions on behalf of mentally incapacitated adults?*

Guidance for deciding what is in a person's "best interests"

3.23. In determining a person's best interests, the Law Commission recommended that regard should be given to the following factors:

> the ascertainable past and present wishes and feelings of the person concerned and the factors the person would consider if able to do so;

> the need to permit and encourage the person to participate or improve his or her ability to participate as fully as possible in anything done for and any decision affecting him or her;

> the views of other people whom it is appropriate and practical to consult about the person's wishes and feelings and what would be in his or her best interests; and

whether the purpose for which any action or decision is required can be as effectively achieved in a manner less restrictive of the person's freedom of action.

These issues, of course, generally are more acute in the field of medical treatment decisions.

3.24. The Government endorses the need for guidance as to the criteria that must be taken into account when a decision-maker is considering what is in a person without capacity's best interests but seeks views on whether the list would prove workable, and useful, in practice. In particular, the medical profession should be cognisant of the possible conflicting roles of informants, including the possibility of disagreements among those who are consulted; the position of medical professionals who fail to make all proper enquiries; and the subjectivity, both of the criteria, and of relatives or carers who are required to make the necessary judgements. In addition, the Government would welcome views on the impact of religious or cultural factors in establishing a person's best interests.

> **Q11.** *Is the proposed guidance for deciding what is in a person's best interests appropriate?*
>
> *In particular:*
>
> i. *how should the decision-maker deal with differences of opinion between those who are to be consulted?*
>
> ii. *will the medical profession be subject to accusations of negligence if they fail to make proper enquiries to identify or locate all interested parties?*
>
> iii. *can we always expect relatives and carers to put the interests of the person without capacity entirely before their own, especially if their own welfare or that of another relative or close friend is at stake?*
>
> iv. *should the guidance take into account religious or cultural factors in establishing a person's best interests? If so, how could this most effectively be done?*

3.25. The Government also notes that a local authority social services department and General Practitioners may have a responsibility towards a relative or carer as well as towards the person without capacity.

GENERAL AUTHORITY TO ACT REASONABLY
Informal decision-making

3.26. There can be no doubt that many decisions are taken every day for people without capacity, with very little authority, whether by carers, family members or treatment providers. This can extend, for example, to paying bills, purchasing necessities, giving medication, dealing with landlords. This substitute authority may develop piecemeal and may become quite extensive before the person without or with limited capacity has a chance to realise how wide this authority has become. This authority may be unregulated in terms of protecting the person without capacity and poses a certain amount of risk for the carer in that they may have little or no legal basis for their actions.

3.27. The Law Commission recommended that this informality of decision-making should remain and that there should not be undue recourse to the courts. They did, however, suggest that these decisions be put in a legal context which gave clarity for the carers and adequate protection for those without capacity.

3.28. The Law Commission recommended that it should be lawful "to do anything for the personal welfare or health care of a person who is, or is reasonably believed to be, without capacity in relation to the matter in question if it is in all the circumstances reasonable for it to be done by the person who does it."[9] Four concepts are included in this paragraph: the first is whether the action undertaken was reasonable; the second is whether it was reasonable for that particular person to undertake the action. The third concept is whether the decision-maker reasonably believes that the person concerned lacked capacity. The fourth concept is a liability of a person who makes a decision in accordance with a general authority. The Law Commission recommends that decisions made in accordance with the requirements of the general authority should be lawful. If a person makes a decision on behalf of a person without capacity in accordance with the general authority then he will not face civil liability – for example, in relation to the tort of trespass to person, or assault as a result of the decision. The Government seeks views on whether the definition of the general authority is appropriate.

> **Q12.** **Is the Law Commission definition of the general authority satisfactory? If not, how should it be amended?**

Capacity to contract

3.29. The common law already provides that where goods or services which are "necessaries" are supplied to a person with a disability then, even if the supplier knew or ought to have known of the disability (and therefore cannot enforce the contract itself) that supplier has the right to recover a reasonable price[10]. The Law Commission recommended incorporating the common law principle of 'necessaries' in their draft Bill. This would mean that where necessary goods are supplied to or necessary services are provided for a person without capacity to contract, he or she should pay a reasonable price for them. This enables people without capacity to be provided with the basic goods and services they might otherwise be deprived of, with the safeguard that the price charged must be reasonable. The Government accepts this recommendation.

3.30. The Law Commission recommended that payment might be made in a number of ways:

> a carer might pay using the person without capacity's money;
>
> a carer might pay and then claim from the person without capacity; or
>
> a promise might be made on behalf of the person without capacity to pay at a later date.

---

9 *Law Com 231, para 4.4.*

10 *See also the Sale of Goods Act 1979, s3(2) which gives the rule statutory form in relation to goods.*

3.31. The Government accepts this recommendation in principle, but has some concerns about whether such a scheme might be open to abuse.

> **Q13a.** **Are additional safeguards required to ensure the "necessaries" rule does not lead to abuses?**

> **Q13b.** **If so, what additional safeguards might be incorporated?**

A release of payments scheme

3.32. The Law Commission suggested a means of ensuring that those caring for a person without capacity can have access to funds to deal with the day-to-day necessities required without continual recourse to the courts. This would enable banks, building societies etc. to make arrangements with carers, once carers had demonstrated that the person in their care did not have capacity. Responses to the Law Commission suggested that an accessible system of this type was needed by carers who otherwise faced delay, cost and lack of legal protection.

3.33. The Law Commission suggested that, on receipt of certification from a medical practitioner that the person concerned did indeed lack capacity, companies might make limited contractual arrangements with a third party for withdrawals on behalf of the person without capacity. Such a provision would be particularly useful where the person without capacity had not indicated a person they would wish to handle their affairs in advance of their incapacity.

3.34. There would be no compulsion on companies or their depositors to participate in the scheme. A release of payments scheme of this nature would be accompanied by a provision to the effect that, if an institution releases payments in accordance with the terms of the scheme, then the institution will be protected from liability to its customer without capacity for having done so. The Law Commission recommended that the protection would not be available where the customer has opted out, by instructing the institution not to enter into such an agreement, nor will it be available where the original customer, at any time when the agreement is in force, informs the institution that a payment is not to be made. Nor should the institution benefit from the protection from liability if there is reasonable cause to believe that the recipient is likely to misapply the money received.

3.35. The Law Commission proposed a number of safeguards, namely that:

> the recipient must acknowledge that he or she: (1) understands the obligation to apply any money in the best interests of the original customer; and (2) is aware that civil or criminal liability may be incurred if the money is misapplied; and (3) is not aware of any other person who has authority to receive the money;

> there would be a financial limit of £2,000 per year (although this would apply per individual agreement);

> the company would not be protected if the maximum amount was breached;

> the appointments would be time limited for two years; and

a person acting under a power of attorney or similar would be able to override other arrangements.

3.36. The Government accepts these recommendations in principle, and believes the proposal would pose no problems with regard to the majority of carers who are likely to act only in the person without capacity's best interests, but there are a number of practical problems, including ensuring that there are adequate safeguards against abuse, on which respondents' views are requested.

> **Q14.** *How would a release of payments scheme work in practice? In particular:*
>
>   *i*   *will sufficient institutions and individuals be willing to participate in the scheme to make it workable?*
>
>   *ii.*   *will there need to be an obligation on companies to check that the information provided is valid?*
>
>   *iii.*   *will doctors fully understand the financial implications of the medical certificate they are preparing?*
>
>   *iv.*   *will there be a need for appropriate witnessing or authorising of the medical certificate to prevent fraud?*
>
>   *v.*   *is the proposed limit of £2000 per year realistic and practical? If not, what should be the limit?*

Direct payments to third parties

3.37. The Law Commission's draft Bill also makes provision for direct payments to third parties. Similar concerns to those outlined above will, however, also apply to this proposal. One way of limiting potential abuse would be to ensure that direct payments could only be made in respect of contracts which related to the necessaries of life e.g. housing costs, water, fuel, food etc.

> **Q15.** *Should direct payments to third parties be restricted to "necessaries" only?*

Alternative Scottish proposals

3.38. The Scottish Law Commission proposed a slightly different scheme that would allow carers to make withdrawals from the bank account of a person without capacity, where authorised to do so by a central authority, the public guardian. Following the consultation exercise earlier in 1997, the Government is now proposing a slightly revised scheme that would operate in Scotland. The Government believes that it would be desirable to adopt a common scheme north and south of the Border, as many banks and other organisations have branches throughout Great Britain and would find it difficult to operate two different schemes.

3.39. The main features of the proposed Scottish scheme are:

> Carers would apply to the public guardian, an officer of the Supreme Court, for authority for single payments, or a series of regular payments, from the bank account of the person without capacity to be made to a specially designated account at the same bank.

The carer would operate the designated account in the normal way and could use it, for example, to withdraw cash or to make direct debit or standing order arrangements, to meet daily living expenses.

The public guardian would authorise the amount and frequency of payments and would monitor, through spot checks, and the investigation of complaints, that funds were used for the benefit of the person without capacity. The public guardian would be able to make enquiries about transactions on the designated account and on the account of the person without capacity.

The public guardian would review the authority to withdraw regularly. He would investigate any problems or suspicious circumstances.

The public guardian would be able to charge a fee.

The bank would be liable to the person without capacity for allowing payments over the limits set out in the public guardian's authority.

Q16. **What are the respective merits of the Law Commission's scheme at paragraphs 3.32 – 3.37 and the Scottish proposals at paragraph 3.39? In particular:**

    i. **is it desirable to have a common scheme for Scotland and England and Wales?**

    ii. **is it desirable to have the additional protection for the funds of the person without capacity that is provided by the public guardian in the Scottish proposals, recognising that the public guardian role will require to be funded?**

    iii. **who would perform the role of the public guardian, should the Scottish proposals be adopted for England and Wales?**

Restrictions on the General Authority

3.40. The Law Commission recommended that a person acting under the general authority should not be able to make a decision on behalf of the person without capacity on the following matters:

consent to marriage;

consent to sexual relations;

consent to divorce on the basis of two years separation (this will become redundant following the implementation of the Family Law Act 1996);

agreement to adoption or consent to freeing a child for adoption;

voting at an election for any public office; or

discharging parental responsibilities, except in relation to a child's property.

3.41. The Government accepts this recommendation in principle, but suggests that, in relation to a child's property, the interests of the child should continue to take precedence over those of the person without capacity. The views of respondents would be welcomed.

> **Q17.** *Should the interests of a child continue to take precedence over those of the person without capacity in relation to a child's property?*

Coercion and Confinement
Harm <u>to</u> a person without capacity

3.42. To ensure that the general authority specifically excluded actions which might infringe the civil liberties of the person without capacity, the Law Commission recommended that the general authority should not include the authorisation of "the use or threat of force to enforce the doing of anything to which that person objects; nor should it authorise the detention or confinement of that person, whether or not he objects. This provision is not to preclude the taking of steps which are necessary to avert a substantial risk of serious harm to the person concerned."[11] Such a provision would also make it clear what action a carer might reasonably take without risk of legal action.

Harm <u>by</u> a person without capacity

3.43. The Law Commission considered that no reference to harm to others is called for in any new statute since this contingency is adequately covered in existing law[12]. This is an issue on which there has been public concern and the Government is of the view that there should be an express statutory provision regarding harm to others which would clarify the legal position.

Decisions of the court or of a person appointed by the court or under a valid power of attorney

3.44. The Law Commission recommended that a decision of the court or of an appointed manager would override this general authority. Where, however, there was a potential conflict, for example a person acting under a general authority disagrees with a person operating under a valid power of attorney, the Law Commission recommended that there should be no restrictions on action being undertaken to prevent the death or serious deterioration of the condition of the person without capacity pending a decision by the court.

3.45. The Government accepts this recommendation in principle.

Code of Practice

3.46. The Law Commission recommended that a Code of Practice on the definition of reasonableness might be helpful to offer further guidance to carers in this area.

3.47. The Government accepts that guidance to professional carers would be helpful, but seeks views on how best to provide guidance for other carers, such as family members.

> **Q18.** *What type of guidance might be helpful for carers?*

---

11 *Law Com 231, para 4.33.*

12 *Ibid., paras 4.30 and 4.31.*

New offence

3.48. The Law Commission recommended that it should be an offence to ill treat or wilfully neglect a person in relation to whom he or she has powers by virtue of the new legislation. Such an offence could only be committed by: any person having the care of, or in lawful control of the property of the person concerned; any donee of a continuing power of attorney; or a court appointed manager. The Law Commission regarded the existing offence under the Mental Health Act as being insufficient. The Government accepts this, given that the categories of person covered by the term "incapacity" are broader under the Law Commission proposals than those covered by the Mental Health Act. The introduction of such an offence would also give a clear message that any new legislation is not only about simplifying the rights of carers – their responsibilities towards the person without capacity are also taken very seriously indeed.

Advance Statements About Health Care

BACKGROUND

4.1. The Law Commission's Report attempts to clarify the legal status of health care decisions which are intended to have effect when a patient loses capacity. Such decisions are often called **advance directives**, or **living wills**. The Law Commission used the term **advance statement**, however, as the terms "advance directive" and "living will" suggest that anticipatory decisions will always be made in writing. That is not always the case. However a decision is communicated, it can specify the types of treatment which a patient would or would not find acceptable in certain circumstances. Where an advance statement is limited to specifying treatment which the patient would not consider acceptable, it is commonly called an **advance refusal**.

4.2. The Government recognises the strength of feeling on this subject. This was the area of the Law Commission's work which aroused the greatest public concern, and it is clear that this is a matter on which many have deep rooted personal, moral, religious and ethical views. The Government does not believe that it would be appropriate to reach any conclusions in this area in the absence of fresh consultation – not just on the detailed plans put forward by the Law Commission, but also on the need for and the merits of legislation in this area generally.

4.3. In seeking views on these issues and on the detail of the Law Commission's recommendations, the Government would wish to clarify two points, about which correspondence received after the publication of the Law Commission's report revealed some misconceptions.

4.4. First, some people thought the Law Commission's recommendations would make legal provision for the first time for advance statements. This is not the case. This misconception seems to be based on the assumption that advance statements have no basis in existing law. In reality, however, *certain forms of advance statement already have full effect at common law*. The judgements in *Re T*[1], together with those in Airedale *NHS Trust v Bland*[2] in both the Court of Appeal and the House of Lords indicate that an advance refusal which is 'clearly established' and 'applicable in the circumstances' is as effective as the decision of a capable adult. The case of *Re C*[3] further clarified the position. As the Law Commission stated in their Report on Mental Incapacity: "An advance refusal made with capacity simply survives any supervening

---

1   *Re T (Adult: Refusal of Treatment) [1992] WLR 782.*

2   *Airedale NHS Trust v Bland [1993] AC 789.*

3   *Re C (Adult Refusal of Treatment) [1994] 1 WLR 290.*

incapacity"[4]. In their evidence to the House of Lords Select Committee on Medical Ethics, the Mental Health and Disability Sub-Committee of the Law Society said that many solicitors are now preparing advance statements on their clients' instructions[5]. The Law Commission proposals thus serve mainly to clarify the existing legal position.

4.5.   The other major misconception is that the Law Commission's proposals would entail the legalisation of euthanasia[6]. As was stated in the introduction to this Paper, the Government fully supports the views of the House of Lords Select Committee on Medical Ethics that euthanasia is unacceptable and the Government has no plans to change this position.

House of Lords Select Committee on Medical Ethics

4.6.   In considering this issue, the Government acknowledges that the House of Lords Select Committee commended the development of advance statements, but decided that "it could well be impossible to give advance statements in general greater legal force without depriving patients of the benefit of the doctor's professional expertise and of new treatments and procedures which may have become available since the directive was signed"[7]. The Committee did, however, suggest that a Code of Practice would be useful. The British Medical Association (BMA) have since produced a Code of Practice on advance statements and a guide for patients was produced in 1996 by the Patients Association in collaboration with the BMA.

4.7.   The Government also supports the efforts of the medical profession to involve patients in all decision-making regarding their treatment as far as this is possible. The Government accepts that this is an evolving area and that current case law is establishing a useful basis on which policy can be developed. There has been relatively little relevant case law as yet, however, and the Code of Practice on Advance Statements is a relatively recent development, so the Government recognises there might be some merit in postponing further policy development in this area, until there has been more of an opportunity to consider the impact of case law and the Code of Practice.

4.8.   Given the importance of this issue, the Government would welcome views on the following questions:

Q19.   Should the Government legislate in the area of advance statements?

Q20.   What should be the objective of legislation on advance statements?

The Law Commission's proposals

4.9.   If it is decided that it would be appropriate to legislate in this area, the detailed proposals of the Law Commission represent an appropriate place from which to take forward further consideration. Consultation on the details of the Law Commission's work should not be seen as prejudicial to the answers to questions 19 and 20, above.

4.10.   The Law Commission drew a distinction between advance *expressions of views and preferences* and advance *decisions*. Briefly, the Law Commission considered that their general proposals on

---

4   *Law Com 231, Para. 5.14.*

5   *HL Paper 21-I, para. 185.*

6   *Euthanasia is defined as a deliberate intervention undertaken with the express intention of ending a life, albeit at the person's own request or for a merciful motive.*

7   *HL Paper 21-I, para. 264.*

mental incapacity would cater for advance expressions of *views*. They therefore concentrated on the position surrounding advance *decisions*.

4.11. As advance decisions *cannot* compel a doctor to provide treatment which they regard as not in the patient's best interests, nor to do anything which is not lawful, the Law Commission decided that the principal problems in this area lay with advance refusals of treatment where such a refusal might go against the views of the health care professionals caring for the patient.

ADVANCE REFUSALS OF TREATMENT

4.12. The present position is that a mentally competent patient has a right to refuse medical treatment for any reason, rational or irrational, or for no reason at all, even when that decision will lead to his or her death. The performance of physically invasive medical treatment without the patient's consent is a criminal or tortious assault. Where the patient does not have the capacity to give consent at the time when it is needed, the doctor can give treatment, in the patient's best interests, which is necessary to save their life, or preserve or prevent a deterioration in their physical or mental health, providing that treatment is not contrary to the known, competent, previously expressed decision of the patient[8]. The doctor must therefore interpret any statements the patient has previously made, whether orally or in writing, and relate them to the treatment contemplated. This may not be easy, especially if new treatments have developed since the advance decision was made or if it is not clear that the patient intended the statement to apply to the treatment being considered.

4.13. The principle which the Law Commission sought to protect was the almost unanimous view of respondents to consultation that "patients should be enabled and encouraged to exercise genuine choice about treatments and procedures". The Government shares this view.

Requests for futile or illegal treatment

4.14. An advance statement cannot:

require a doctor to do anything which is not lawful, including taking steps purely to end the patient's life; or

make a doctor provide treatment which the doctor regards as not in a patient's best interests.

4.15. It will thus be impossible for an advance statement by someone who has since lost capacity to have this effect. Advance statements cannot require or allow a doctor to participate in "mercy" killing. This will remain an offence of murder. The Government has no plans to change this position.

Acting reasonably in a patient's best interests

4.16. In general, the Law Commission recommended that decisions relating to medical treatment on behalf of a person without capacity should be made in the person's best interests. The fact that the best interests will include their "past and present wishes and feelings and the factors he or she would consider" will ensure that their wishes are routinely taken into account.

---

8 Treatment can, however, be given for mental disorder under the Mental Health Act 1983 if the relevant criteria are met.

4.17. With regard to advance consents to treatment, the Law Commission thought that these best interests criteria would meet the concerns of the House of Lords Select Committee on Medical Ethics that a patient might be deprived of a new treatment, of which he or she was perhaps unaware when an advance statement was signed. For example, the doctor would be obliged to consider whether the patient intended the advance statement applying in all the circumstances of the case or whether the new treatment is something they would have wished to consider had they known about it. If the patient has lost capacity the doctor can still be helped in reaching his or her decision by the views of other appropriate people, such as family or other carers. The best interests criteria also oblige the doctor to encourage the patient to participate in treatment decisions as long as he or she is able. This should ensure that, where possible, doctors discuss advances in treatment with their patients so that a patient has the opportunity to make an informed choice about whether he or she wishes to change their mind or modify their advance statement. The Law Commission made it clear, however, that if an advance refusal has been made, then a treatment provider cannot rely on the authority which would otherwise enable a patient without capacity to be treated reasonably and in his or her best interests.

4.18. The advance statement is not, therefore, to be seen in isolation, but against a background of doctor/patient dialogue and the involvement of other carers who may be able to give an insight as to what the patient would want in the particular circumstances of the case. Codes of Practice and Guidance for Patients will also help here.

> **Q21. Would the safeguards be sufficient to ensure that advance statements did not unintentionally prevent the use of medical procedures developed since the drafting of the statement?**

Anticipatory decisions by patients

4.19. As has been said above, the Law Commission found that most problems in this area related to where patients had made an advance decision to refuse treatment. Where there is no advance statement or an advance statement giving consent, the treatment will be carried out where it is in the patient's best interests. A doctor is put into a more difficult position where the decision to refuse treatment is against his or her professional judgement.

4.20. The Law Commission thus recommended that an advance refusal be defined as "a refusal made by a person aged 18 or over with the necessary capacity of any medical, surgical or dental treatment or other procedure and intended to have effect at any subsequent time when he or she may be without capacity to give or refuse consent"[9].

4.21. The Law Commission did not include under 18 year olds, because in this area it is accepted case law that the inherent jurisdiction of the court and a person exercising parental responsibility can overrule this choice[10].

> **Q22. Is this an appropriate definition of an advance refusal?**

---

9 Law Com 231, para. 5.16.

10 See Re R [1991] 4 All ER 177; Re W [1993] Fam 64.

Necessary capacity

4.22. While it may seem straightforward in principle, the question of 'necessary capacity' is a complex one. Some patients do not wish to be told the extent of their illness or of the repercussions of a failure to undertake treatment. Although some may argue that this refusal to hear all medical advice is also one of choice, it nevertheless makes it difficult for a doctor to be sure that the person fully understands the implications of an advance refusal.

4.23. Advance statements may thus need to be subject to certain safeguards, namely that the patient has been given the relevant information to make an informed choice. The Government would be concerned to ensure that advance statements are not made in cases where people do not fully understand the implications of their decision. It is important, however, to ensure that any system is not unnecessarily formal and hence restrictive of patient choice.

Q23. **How best could safeguards be put in place to ensure advance statements are the result of a choice that is informed, considered, and free from undue influence?**

Terminal conditions

4.24. The Law Commission recommended that advance refusals should be accepted in all and not just terminal conditions, as this would otherwise undermine the principle that people with capacity should be able to refuse any treatment in advance of a time where they might subsequently lose this capacity. The Government accepts that there are risks in restricting the potential applicability of advance refusals: such a move would restrict, for example, healthy fit people from making an advance statement to say that were they to suffer the misfortune of being involved in a traffic accident, or involved in a situation akin to the Hillsborough disaster, they would not wish to be kept alive in a persistent vegetative state.

4.25. The Law Commission also recommended that this refusal should continue to apply where someone had been granted a general authority to act in the event of a person losing capacity, so that they should not be able to overrule a patient's clearly stated advance decision on medical treatment. This would also relieve some people acting under a general authority from the distress of having to implement any decision with which they disagreed, although the Government would be concerned to ensure that the advance statement was not able to rule out the possibility of someone acting with general authority from making a decision based on more recent developments in medical procedure if, having regard to the previously expressed wishes of the person it would appear to be in their best interests to do so.

Q24. **Should advance refusals apply to all cases?**

Q25. **If in general advance statements overrule the decision-making of someone granted general authority, in what circumstances (if any) should there be an exception to this rule?**

Life-sustaining treatment

4.26. The Law Commission recommended that an advance refusal should be presumed not to apply where the life of the patient or, if the patient is pregnant, the life of the foetus is in danger. Any person who wishes the advance refusal to apply, even if this would result in death, will thus need to make sure this is explicitly stated. This can arise now, for example Jehovah's Witnesses refusing blood and in the case of *Re C*[11], where a man refused amputation, even though doctors believed he would die without such treatment.

4.27. This provides a safeguard that the life of the patient will always be preserved in matters of doubt. However, it would be necessary to ensure that any person who wished to make an advance refusal explicitly acknowledges that death could be a consequence of their refusal.

> **Q26.** **Should an advance refusal only apply when the life of the patient is in danger if the refusal has specifically acknowledged the risk of death?**

Pregnant women

4.28. The Law Commission recommended that a woman's right to determine the sorts of bodily interference which she will tolerate should not evaporate merely because she is pregnant. The Government accepts this recommendation in principle.

4.29. The Law Commission also recommended, however, that an advance refusal should only apply where the woman has explicitly referred to the fact that the refusal should continue to apply despite her pregnancy. This might affect refusals made in contemplation of a wide range of circumstances. On the one hand, this might affect a long standing advance refusal concerning treatment the woman would wish to receive should she be suffering from a persistent vegetative state. However, some refusals may be made during pregnancy in contemplation of treatment during labour, for example to refuse a caesarean section. In certain circumstances, caesarean section may be necessary in labour to save the life of the woman. In relation to life sustaining treatment the Law Commission, as noted in paragraphs 4.26 and 4.27 above, recommended safeguards to ensure that the life of the patient will always be preserved in matters of doubt. Although views have been sought on the general principle of advance statements having application only when the risk of death has been specifically acknowledged, the Government would also welcome views on whether in the circumstances of childbirth an advance refusal of treatment would need specifically to acknowledge such a risk.

> **Q27a.** **Should a woman need to refer specifically to pregnancy in order for an advance refusal to apply during pregnancy?**

> **Q27b.** **Should advance refusals concerning treatment in childbirth only apply when the life of the patient is in danger if the refusal has specifically acknowledged the risk of death?**

---

11 *Re C [1994] 1 WLR 290.*

Liability of health care providers

4.30. The Law Commission recommended that the legal position of health care professionals be clarified, where they either withhold treatment where they understand that this would accord with a patient's wishes, or where they proceed with treatment only to find that, unknown to them, the patient did not wish this. The Law Commission's recommendations make it clear that no person should incur liability in either of these circumstances – for example, where health care professionals proceed with medical treatment in circumstances where they did not know of the existence of an advance refusal or have reasonable grounds to believe that one existed, and then an advance refusal is found, they should still be prevented from incurring liability in the law of tort (for example for trespass to person) providing the decision to give the treatment was made in accordance with the Law Commission's recommendations. It would be the responsibility of the person making an advance refusal to ensure that the existence of the refusal comes to the notice of the treatment provider. This clarifies the existing law.

Q28. **Would these recommendations provide an appropriate balance between protecting health care providers, and protecting patients?**

The form of an advance refusal

4.31. The current common law position is that it is the "true scope and basis" of the decision rather than the way it has been recorded which is of importance in determining the validity of an advance refusal.

4.32. Both the BMA and the Law Society recommended that there should be maximum flexibility in drawing up an advance refusal so that a patient's wishes were not overridden simply because they were recorded in the wrong format. The Law Commission did not suggest that an advance statement had to be made in a prescribed manner but recommended that an advance refusal should be presumed to be validly made if, in the absence of any indication to the contrary, it is in writing, signed and witnessed.

4.33. Advance refusals of treatment will not always exist in such a form. In the field of palliative care, for example, there is an ongoing dialogue between patient and doctor as to the treatment the patient wishes to have as their illness progresses. These views may be recorded in the patient's notes.

Q29. **In what form or forms should an advance statement be recorded in order to be valid?**

Withdrawing or altering an advance refusal

4.34. One concern which has been persistently raised in relation to advance refusals of treatment is what happens if the person changes their mind. The Law Commission recommended that the person who made the advance refusal should be able to withdraw or alter it at any time that they have the capacity to do so. The Government agrees.

Exclusion of basic care

4.35. The Law Commission recommended that an advance refusal of treatment should never be able to include a refusal of "basic care". This care includes that to maintain bodily cleanliness, alleviation of severe pain and the provision of direct oral nutrition and hydration.

4.36. It was thought that it would place an intolerable burden on nursing staff if such care could be withheld and such a withdrawal of care might also have implications for other patients, particularly where bodily hygiene was concerned.

4.37. Although the general authority proposed by the Law Commission did not extend to the authorisation of the use or threat of force, their proposals did not preclude the taking of steps which are necessary to avert a substantial risk of serious harm to the person concerned. In certain circumstances, therefore, for people who had made advance refusals who were suffering from a terminal illness or were in the last stages of a hunger strike and had lost competence, the proposals might mean that such people would need to be administered direct oral nutrition and hydration by force against their objections. Although the Government would in principle agree that direct oral nutrition or hydration should always be offered, it is concerned at the prospect of forced oral feeding.

Q30. *Should an advance refusal be able to refuse "basic care"?*

Q31. *How should "basic care" be defined?*

Q32. *Should a person who has made an appropriate advance refusal be administered direct oral nutrition and hydration against their objections (force fed)?*

RESORT TO THE COURTS

4.38. The Law Commission recommended that recourse to the courts should only be available and necessary where a decision is required about the validity or applicability of an advance refusal or a question as to whether or not it had been withdrawn. The Law Commission recommended that, where there was any lack of clarity, the existence of the advance refusal should not preclude any treatment to prevent the death or serious deterioration of the patient pending a decision of the court as to the validity or applicability of the advance refusal. This reflects the current position and ensures that lives are not lost as a result of a misunderstanding of a patient's intentions.

Q33. *Would the courts be the most appropriate forum for deciding on the validity or applicability of an advance statement?*

Concealing or destroying a document

4.39   The Law Commission recommended that it should be an offence punishable with a maximum of two years imprisonment to conceal or destroy a written advance refusal of treatment with intent to deceive. This was not unanimously accepted on consultation, with some experts believing that the existing criminal law would cover such offences. The Law Commission considered that it was not clear that the existing criminal law would cover concealment or destruction of a written advance refusal with intent to deceive the treatment provider. The creation of a new offence would also ensure that the importance of the advance statement was recognised and that there was clarity about the repercussions. The Government seeks views on this conclusion.

Q34.   *Should there be a specific offence of concealing or destroying a written advance refusal of treatment with intent to deceive?*

Independent Supervision of Medical and Research Procedures

BACKGROUND

5.1. The Law Commission thought that certain types of serious medical procedures, including sterilisation, donation of tissue or bone marrow, and abortion, should be subject to additional independent supervision to ensure that the best interests of the person without capacity are protected. In some exceptional instances there might also be situations where the person's best interests are not the only consideration.

5.2. The Law Commission recommended that decisions on some procedures should be either:

> considered by the courts;
>
> the subject of an independent second medical opinion;
>
> the subject of consideration by the court or the second opinion procedure; or
>
> (in relation to certain types of research) subject to another kind of supervisory mechanism.

5.3. The Law Commission recommended that where there was a valid advance statement, or a power of attorney covering the specific issue in question or the court had appointed a manager to deal with the particular decision, the special procedures might not be necessary and hence their recommendations integrate these other methods of decision making into their proposals in these areas.

5.4. The Government accepts the principle behind many of the recommendations made in these areas, but seeks views on how the proposals would work in practice. This chapter, however, also sets out a number of key ethical issues, on which the Government would welcome views as to whether the Law Commission's recommendations are appropriate.

5.5. Consideration of the procedures discussed in this chapter is most likely to arise in relation to those whose incapacity is expected to be prolonged or permanent. Where a person is likely to recover capacity, making a treatment decision that is relatively irrevocable, such as that concerning sterilisation other than in the case of necessity to treat a disease, is likely to be inappropriate.

TREATMENTS REQUIRING COURT APPROVAL

5.6. Respondents to the Law Commission's consultation were unanimous in agreeing that some medical decisions should always require prior judicial approval. The court could achieve this by making a one-off decision or by appointing a manager to take the decision in question. The Law Commission recommended that the court need not be involved if the person without capacity had appointed an attorney to take the decision on his or her behalf and the power of attorney specifically covered the issues subject to this special procedure[1]. They recommended that the general authority to act reasonably should not be able to authorise any treatments or procedures which required the authorisation of the court or the consent of an attorney or manager.

5.7. The Government has some doubts about whether an attorney should be able to consent to medical procedures which would otherwise require court approval. Under the ethical codes of the medical profession, doctors will only offer treatment if they perceive it to be in a patient's best interests to receive it. There is no question of doctors being forced to offer treatment if they do not believe it to be in a patient's best interests. An attorney therefore has to form his or her own view of the patient's best interests. If that view is that the proposed treatment is in the patient's best interests, the attorney will agree with the doctor and consent. If the attorney disagrees that the treatment is in the patient's best interests, he will wish to refuse the treatment. Were this not to be permitted, the matter might then need to be considered by the court. In such a situation, it would appear that the attorney is in some sense acting as a double check in that his powers only extend to agreeing with the doctor.

> **Q35.** *Should an attorney be able to consent to medical procedures which would otherwise require the approval of the court?*
>
> **Q36.** *Should an attorney ever be able to refuse treatment?*

Sterilisation

5.8. The Law Commission separated sterilisations into three categories, those required:

> to treat a disease of the reproductive organs;
>
> to relieve an existing detrimental effect of menstruation; and
>
> to deal with contraception.

5.9. The Law Commission recommended that any treatment or procedure intended or reasonably likely to render the person permanently infertile should require court authorisation unless it is to treat a disease of the reproductive organs or relieve existing detrimental effects of menstruation. They noted that none of their respondents had suggested that judicial supervision was necessary in respect of treatment of a disease of the reproductive organs. The Government notes that treatment of diseases other than those affecting the reproductive organs, such as chemotherapy for cancer, may be likely to render a person permanently infertile. This issue is therefore considered both in this section, in the context of treatments requiring court approval, and in the next section, which looks at procedures which require a second doctor's certificate.

---

1 *Consideration of the Law Commission's recommendations relating to powers of attorney is given in Chapter 6. See in particular the requirement for an attorney to act in a person's best interests in paragraph 6.17.*

5.10. The Government recognises the sensitivity of this subject, and is particularly concerned that legislation on sterilisation should be accompanied by appropriate safeguards.

> ***Q37a.*** ***Should the court be asked to rule on all proposed sterilisations for contraceptive purposes?***
>
> ***Q37b.*** ***Should the court be asked to rule on all proposed sterilisations to relieve the existing detrimental effects of menstruation?***
>
> ***Q37c.*** ***Should the court be asked to rule on all treatment for diseases where the treatment will, or is reasonably likely to, render the person permanently infertile?***

Donation of tissue or bone marrow

5.11. The Law Commission recommended that any treatment or procedure to facilitate the donation of non-regenerative tissue or bone marrow should require court authorisation. Organ donation will rarely seem in the best interests of the person without capacity, but could have long-term implications for them, for example if the person who requires the organ is a close family relative who has caring responsibilities for the person without capacity.

5.12. Since the publication of the Law Commission's Report, the judgement in *Re Y*[2] has clarified that, under existing common law, any proposal for bone marrow donation from an adult incapable of giving consent must first be aired in the courts, who will consider whether such a procedure would be lawful in the individual circumstances of the case.

5.13. The Government accepts the principle, and the current common law position, that the court should rule on any treatment or procedure to facilitate donation of non-regenerative tissue or bone marrow from an adult incapable of giving consent. Again, however, the Government is concerned to ensure that adequate safeguards are in place. Accordingly it seeks the views of respondents on whether there should be procedural safeguards for the donation of any other organs or tissue. This may include regenerative tissue, other than bone marrow, such as blood. We note that for blood, current guidance issued by the National Blood Service stresses that collection teams should screen out any adult who they consider is incapable of understanding the information with which they are provided. Conversely, views are also sought on whether any non-regenerative tissues or bone marrow should be excluded from the general rule.

> ***Q38.*** ***Should the donation of any organs be excluded from this general rule?***
>
> ***Q39a.*** ***Should it ever be necessary to consider an incapacitated person as a donor of regenerative tissue?***
>
> ***Q39b.*** ***If so, should there be procedural safeguards similar to those which exist for non-regenerative tissue or bone marrow?***

---

2 *Re Y [1997] 2 WLR 556.*

Power to prescribe further treatments

5.14. The Law Commission suggested that the Secretary of State for Health should have the power to prescribe further treatments which required court authorisation to ensure that any changes in medical science would not require the amendment of primary legislation.

5.15. The Government agrees with this recommendation.

TREATMENTS REQUIRING A SECOND DOCTOR'S CERTIFICATE

5.16. The Law Commission thought that a second opinion procedure would sometimes be more appropriate than court proceedings. This would be consistent with the treatments for mental disorder specified in section 58 of the Mental Health Act 1983. The types of decisions the Law Commission recommended for inclusion in this category relate to a medical complaint from which the person without capacity is already suffering. The doctor giving the second opinion would be required to certify whether the person had the capacity to understand the implications of the treatment and consequently make a decision about whether to consent to or refuse it; and whether the treatment or procedure proposed was indeed in the patient's best interests.

5.17. The Law Commission thought that this procedure would be unnecessary where a donee of a power of attorney or a court appointed manager could make the decision. They recommended that the general authority to act reasonably should not be able to authorise treatments specified as requiring a certificate from an independent doctor appointed for that purpose by the Secretary of State. This should not prevent action being taken to prevent the death of the patient or serious deterioration in his or her condition while the certification or consent is being sought.

Sterilisation

5.18. The Law Commission recommended that any treatment or procedure likely to render the person concerned permanently infertile should require a certificate from an independent medical practitioner where it is for relieving the existing detrimental effects of menstruation. The Government wishes to ensure that sufficient safeguards are provided, and question 37, above, has sought views on whether the court should take responsibility for such decisions.

Abortion

5.19. The Law Commission recommended that the second opinion procedure should also apply where abortion was being considered. The current law already requires two doctors to certify in good faith that the statutory grounds for abortion are met.

5.20. The Government considers that the existing legislation provides an acceptable framework for decision-making in this area. Consideration will be given as to whether practice can be improved within the current statutory framework.

Treatments for Mental Disorder

5.21. The Law Commission also recommended that such a procedure should apply when it is proposed to administer medical treatment for mental disorder described in section 58(1) of the Mental Health Act 1983 where the person does not have capacity to consent to that treatment.

The Law Commission preferred this option to suggesting that patients should always be detained and treated under the Mental Health Act as this might increase the number of people compulsorily detained. Certain forms of treatment may be given under the Mental Health Act without the consent of the patient, but the doctor is still required by the Mental Health Act Code of Practice to try to obtain consent. The Law Commission regarded a written advance refusal of treatment to be as valid as an oral refusal given at the time the treatment is proposed. Only if the statutory criteria are met could the person be lawfully detained and treated under the Mental Health Act 1983. The Government supports this recommendation.

Q40. **Do the proposals for a second medical opinion provide a sufficient safeguard in relation to:**

    i. **sterilisation to relieve the existing detrimental effects of menstruation;**

    ii. **abortion; or**

    iii. **medical treatment for mental disorder?**

5.22. The Law Commission also proposed that the Secretary of State for Health should be able to add to the list of procedures to be included in the second opinion category.

Q41. **The Government would welcome views on other procedures which should be added to the list proposed by the Law Commission.**

DEPARTING FROM THE BEST INTERESTS CRITERIA

5.23. The Law Commission also recommended that there are certain exceptional situations where a departure from the best interests criteria can be justified.

Withdrawing artificial nutrition and hydration

5.24. The majority of respondents to the Law Commission proposals believed that any decision to withdraw artificial feeding from a patient in a persistent vegetative state should require the prior approval of the court. The Law Commission thought that the main difficulties here lay in withdrawing treatment rather than commencing it, as the best interests criteria would clearly apply in deciding whether a particular course of action, such as an operation to allow direct feeding, would be appropriate[3]. The question to be determined for PVS patients already being provided with artificial hydration and nutrition is, if the patient has any interests at all, whether such treatment is in their best interests. The Law Commission thus recommended that discontinuing the artificial nutrition and hydration of a patient who is 'unconscious, has no activity in the cerebral cortex and no prospect of recovery should be lawful if certain statutory requirements are met'[4].

---

3 *The House of Lords Select Committee on Medical Ethics offered a different view. Pointing out that in many cases it would not be possible to give full consideration to the best interests criteria when commencing treatment (for example in an emergency), the Select Committee concluded "for most practical purposes we do not discern any significant ethical difference between those decisions which involve discontinuing a treatment already begun and those which involve not starting a treatment" – HL Report 21-I, para. 251.*

4 *Law Com 231, para. 6.20.*

5.25. The Government notes the 1996 report of the Royal College of Physicians on the persistent vegetative state[5] which found that there was no evidence that electroencephalography, which measures activity in the cerebral cortex, provided evidence which could improve upon the clinical diagnosis of permanent vegetative state. Such patients may show low levels of activity in the cerebral cortex. The Government therefore seeks views on the following definition:

"patients who have no prospect of recovery who are either unconscious or in a permanent vegetative state".

> **Q42.** **Should the discontinuation of artificial nutrition and hydration be lawful for defined patients if certain statutory criteria are met?**

> **Q43.** **Is "patients who have no prospect of recovery who are either unconscious or in a permanent vegetative state" a suitable definition?**

5.26. The Law Commission suggested that advance refusal of artificial nutrition or hydration could validly be made. The Law Commission also recommended that such a decision could also be taken by a person acting under a power of attorney. A patient could not, however, refuse by advance directive direct oral nutrition or hydration as this would fall within the definition of basic care. The Government agrees that direct oral nutrition and hydration should always be offered, but is concerned to avoid the possibility of force feeding.

5.27. The Law Commission thought that there might come a time when a sufficient bank of case law had been established to allow such decisions to be made under the second opinion procedure rather than by the court. Any such change would only be effected after consultation and following an affirmative resolution of each House of Parliament. Any case of dispute could still be referred to the courts if necessary.

5.28. The Government would welcome views on whether these recommendations, and in particular the recommendation that a power of attorney should be able to confer the right to direct the withdrawal of artificial nutrition or hydration, offer sufficient safeguards for the patient. An alternative would be for all such cases to be decided by the courts. While such a proposal would have clear resource implications, the Government would welcome views on whether such a step is necessary. The Government agrees that an affirmative resolution of both Houses of Parliament should precede any move to allow decisions to withdraw artificial nutrition and hydration to be made under the second opinion procedure rather than by the court, but would welcome views as to whether it is likely that any move in this direction would be appropriate, and whether any additional safeguards would need to be provided.

> **Q44a.** **Should the court retain the exclusive right to make decisions on the withdrawal of artificial nutrition or hydration; or**

> **Q44b.** **Should a person acting under a power of attorney be able to make such decisions? or**

---

5 *Review of a Working group convened by the Royal College of Physicians and endorsed by the Conference of Medical Royal Colleges and their Faculties of the United Kingdom: The Permanent Vegetative State Journal of the Royal College of Physicians of London (1996) 30 (2) 119-121.*

Q44c. *Could these decisions appropriately be made by the second opinion procedure?*

Q45. *If either of the alternatives to the court retaining exclusive rights is considered appropriate, are any additional safeguards necessary in order to protect the patient?*

5.29. The Law Commission recommended that, although the patient in PVS might not technically have any best interests, the factors included in the best interests checklist might nevertheless be valid e.g. the wishes and feelings of the patient and those near to him or her.

5.30. The Government notes the alternative view that such patients do have best interests. This view makes it even more important that each of the best interests criteria must be considered in every case.

Q46. *In considering the continuance or withdrawal from PVS patients of artificial nutrition and hydration, should regard be given to the best interests guidance?*

Procedures to benefit others

5.31. The second area in which the Law Commission thought there might be a case for departing from the best interests criteria is to facilitate procedures for the benefit of others.

5.32. The Law Commission recommended that the Secretary of State for Health might make an order providing for the carrying out of a procedure in relation to a person without capacity to consent, if the procedure, although not carried out for the benefit of that person, will not cause him or her significant harm and will be of significant benefit to others. The Law Commission were not wholly convinced that the case for this change had been proved, particularly as they had not specifically asked for comments on this issue, but they thought that it might become necessary in the future. Any such order should not be made before there had been thorough consultation and the patient should be able to object, for example through an advance refusal or an attorney. Any order made by the Secretary of State would need to specify whether court authorisation or an independent second opinion procedure should apply.

5.33. This recommendation would cover procedures such as genetic screening, which involves taking a sample of blood or other bodily fluids from the patient in order to investigate the genetic make up of that person. This might have significant benefit for other members of the patient's family e.g. to see if a debilitating condition is likely to be inherited, to assist in determining treatment options and enabling that person to make decisions about their future care and reproductive choices. A further procedure is elective ventilation, where an unconscious patient whose death is regarded as inevitable, is ventilated mechanically to enable the retrieval and transplantation of donor organs to take place after death. This benefits the recipients of any organs received. However, there are also potential problems for the patient, their relatives and the wider public. The procedure by which the patient is ventilated may result in the patient entering the persistent vegetative state, which is not in their interests nor in those of relatives. Further, any publicity surrounding this area, which many people find an uncomfortable subject, may impact adversely on organ donation rates. Both of these procedures are currently unlawful.

5.34. This is potentially a wide-ranging recommendation, and, given that the Law Commission did not specifically consult on this issue, the Government would particularly welcome views on the following:

> **Q47.** **Are there any circumstances in which it is ethical and reasonable to apply to patients unable to give consent medical procedures of benefit to others?**

RESEARCH PROCEDURES NOT INTENDED TO BENEFIT THE PARTICIPANT

5.35. Although it may be in a patient's best interests to participate in research which may benefit him or her, this cannot be said to be the case where the research is non-therapeutic i.e. the patient will not benefit directly. If a patient does not have the capacity to consent, any researcher who touches or restrains that person in the course of research will be committing an assault. The research may, however, be of benefit in understanding better the condition from which the patient suffers and may assist future sufferers. The consensus on consultation was that such research could be justifiable where it was concerned with the condition from which the person without capacity suffered and the procedures involved minimal risk and invasiveness. The Law Commission thus recommended that research could be carried out as long as it was into the condition from which the patient suffered and certain statutory procedures were followed.

5.36. The Law Commission recommended that the research involved need not be purely medical but that it would need to satisfy the following:

> that it is desirable to provide knowledge of the causes or treatment of, or of the care of people affected by, the incapacitating condition with which any participant is or may be affected;

> that the object of the research cannot be effectively achieved without the participation of persons who are or may be without the capacity to consent; and

> that the research will not expose a participant to more than negligible risk, will not be unduly invasive or restrictive of a participant and will not unduly interfere with a participant's freedom of action or privacy.

Council of Europe Convention on Human Rights and Biomedicine

5.37. The Council of Europe Convention on Human Rights and Biomedicine recognised that non-therapeutic research on a person not able to consent could be ethical if strict safeguards were provided. Such research must fulfil the general safeguards for any form of research on a person not able to consent, which are that:

> there is no alternative of comparable effectiveness to research on humans;

> the risks which may be incurred by that person are not disproportionate to the potential benefits of that research;

the research project has been approved by a competent body after independent examination of its scientific merit, including assessment of the importance of the aim of the research, and multidisciplinary review of its ethical acceptability (in England and Wales this role would be fulfilled by either the Multi-Centre Research Ethics Committees; the Local Research Ethics Committees; the Gene Therapy Advisory Committee (GTAC); or the United Kingdom Xenotransplantation Interim Regulatory Authority (UKXIRA));

research of comparable effectiveness cannot be carried out on individuals capable of giving consent;

authorisation has been given in the manner provided for by law after relevant information has been given; and

the person concerned does not object.

5.38. As well as these general conditions, non-therapeutic research must also meet the following additional conditions:

the research has the aim of contributing, through significant improvement in the scientific understanding of the individual's condition, disease or disorder, to the ultimate attainment of results conferring benefit on the person concerned or on other persons in the same age category or afflicted with the same disease or disorder or having the same condition; and

the research entails only minimal risk and minimal burden for the individual concerned.[6]

5.39. The Government recognises the high level of feeling about the ethical implications of the Law Commission's recommendations, and the work of the Council of Europe in this area, and therefore seeks views on whether such research should be acceptable, and, if so, on what safeguards could be employed to ensure no abuse of such a scheme.

> **Q48. Should research procedures not intended to benefit the patient be allowed?**

> **Q49. Are the safeguards proposed by the Council of Europe adequate to ensure that any scheme would not be open to abuse?**

> **Q50. What, if any, additional safeguards would be required?**

MENTAL INCAPACITY RESEARCH COMMITTEE

5.40. The Law Commission recommended the establishment of a statutory Mental Incapacity Research Committee which would authorise particular research projects (although further authorisation would be required regarding the participation of particular individuals).

5.41. If safeguards with which research projects must comply are provided by law, the Government is not convinced that an additional committee is required to supplement the established system of Local Research Ethics Committees and the newly developed system of Multi-Centre Research Ethics Committees.

6   *Convention for the Protection of Human Rights and Dignity of the Human Being with Regard to the Application of Biology and Medicine: Convention on Human Rights and Biomedicine, Articles 16 and 17.*

5.42. The Law Commission recommended that, once the research was authorised by the Committee, there was a need for a separate individualised and independent check to confirm whether any particular proposed participant should indeed be brought into the project. In each case the researcher would have to ascertain whether the proposed participant had the capacity to consent. If they did not, then an independent check would be required. This could be by means of obtaining the consent of an attorney or court-appointed manager specifically authorised to make a decision on this matter; a certificate from a doctor not involved in the research that participation was appropriate; or the approval of the court (this would be most likely to occur where there was some disagreement, for example between a family member and an attorney); or, in rare cases the research was authorised as not involving direct contact between researcher and participant – such as covert observation of a patient.

5.43. An advance refusal would prohibit the patient's participation, as would any indication that he or she objects. Regard would be given to the best interests guidance in consideration of the particular circumstances of the case.

5.44. If a decision is taken to legislate in this area, the Government would accept the recommendation that a patient's objection should prohibit participation, which would provide an extra safeguard to help ensure that research is only carried out in appropriate cases.

> **Q51. What benefits would a Mental Incapacity Research Committee provide over and above that provided by Local and Multi-Centre Research Ethics Committees?**

chapter

Continuing Powers of Attorney

BACKGROUND

6.1. The Law Commission's prime objective in this area was "to encourage people to take for themselves those decisions which they are able to take"[1]. The Government fully supports this approach.

6.2. Powers of attorney already exist which allow for decisions to be taken on a person's behalf. The decision as to whether a power of attorney is to be given is one entirely for the donor, provided he or she fully understands the implications of what they are doing and the nature of the document they are signing.

6.3. There are two types of power of attorney:

firstly, an ordinary power of attorney, which can be given by a donor to an attorney or donee to deal with their financial affairs generally, or which can limit authority to specific matters. However, an ordinary power of attorney is automatically revoked by law when the donor loses his or her mental capacity to manage and administer his or her own property and affairs and accordingly the attorney's authority to act under the power ceases; and

secondly, an Enduring Power of Attorney (EPA). This form of power of attorney came into existence in 1986 following the passing of the Enduring Powers of Attorney Act 1985. This Act enabled people to decide who should look after their property and/or financial affairs if they became mentally incapable. Unlike the ordinary power of attorney, an EPA may continue in force after the donor has lost his or her mental capacity to manage and administer his or her financial affairs, provided it has been registered with the Public Trust Office.

The Law Commission's proposals

6.4. The Law Commission's proposals for continuing powers of attorney (CPA) are designed to build on the existing arrangements for powers of attorney, and to enable a person with capacity to set out instructions with regard to the decisions they wish to be made and the person they wish to make them at a time when they might subsequently lose capacity. The Law

---

1 *Law Com 231, para. 7.1.*

Commission regarded judicial intervention as a last resort, but they were concerned that there should be adequate protection for the donor of the power of attorney.

CONTINUING POWERS OF ATTORNEY – DEFINITION AND RESTRICTIONS

6.5. At present powers of attorney can deal only with property matters. The Law Commission recommended that, under its revised and comprehensive code on mental incapacity, there was a need for a form of power of attorney to be made with regard to personal and health care matters as well as property and finance. They thus recommended that a continuing power of attorney should be introduced to cover these areas also. This could grant the donee the authority to make decisions in all areas, including where the donor subsequently loses capacity.

6.6. The Law Commission's proposals that a CPA should be able to extend to matters regarding health, personal welfare and property and affairs (including the conduct of legal proceedings)[2] were unanimously supported on consultation.

House of Lords Select Committee

6.7. The House of Lords Select Committee took a different view in relation to proxy decision-making on health care matters, observing that, 'whilst the idea of the patient-appointed proxy is in many ways attractive, it is vulnerable to the same problems as advance directives, and indeed to a greater degree'[3]. The Committee observed that personal relationships are not immutable, and that the choice of proxy might soon become out of date. In addition the Committee pointed out the practical difficulties of ascertaining what choice the patient would have made, and observed that previous statements of preference form an unreliable basis for future decisions.

6.8. A further point raised by the Select Committee was the difficulty in ensuring the objectivity of the surrogate decision-maker (even when acting in good faith). The Select Committee therefore did not favour the more widespread development of such a system.

6.9. On balance, the Government feels that the Law Commission's proposals contain sufficient safeguards to overcome many of the reservations expressed by the Select Committee. However, given these diverging views, the Government seeks views on whether it would be appropriate to legislate in this area.

Q52. *Should the Government legislate to create a power of attorney so that the attorney is able to make decisions on health care and personal welfare matters?*

6.10. The rest of this chapter invites views on the Law Commission's proposals, including those relating to decision-making on health care matters. This should not be seen as an indication that the Government has decided to pursue this option.

---

2 *The Law Commission listed a number of areas in which they thought an attorney should not be able to act on behalf of a person without capacity: (1) consent to marriage; (2) consent to have sexual relations; (3) consent to a divorce petition on the basis of two years separation; (4) agreement to adoption or consent to freeing a child for adoption; (5) voting at an election for any public office or (6) discharging parental responsibilities except in relation to a child's property.*

3 *HL Paper 21-I, para. 268.*

Decision-making by the donor

6.11. The Law Commission thought that the existence of a CPA should not prevent a person with limited capacity from being able to undertake functions of which he or she is capable, even if in some areas, this overlaps with the authority of the donee. They did not see the necessity for any restrictions on the action of the donor in such circumstances, as long as he or she has the capacity to make the decision in question.

6.12. The Government has some concerns about the practical implications of this proposal, and suggests a possible need for further safeguards to ensure the donee of a CPA does not use this authority unnecessarily where the donor retains capacity for particular decisions.

6.13. An attorney would incur civil liability where he breaches his duties as an attorney. For example, where he makes a decision which is outside the scope of the powers granted to him. The Law Commission recommended that the court should have power to relieve the attorney from some or all of his liabilities. In addition, where the attorney acts in accordance with the power without the knowledge that the donor has revoked it, the attorney is also to be protected. An innocent attorney is also to have protection where he relies on an invalid registered power of attorney.

6.14. Health care providers are to receive some protection if they act on a decision by an attorney which has been revoked and the revocation is unknown to them. They are not, however, to receive special protection from civil liability because they have acted in accordance with an attorney's decision. Health care providers are also to have protection where they rely on a decision made in accordance with an invalid registered power of attorney.

6.15. The Government considers that where an attorney consents to medical treatment which health care providers consider should be given to the patient in accordance with their clinical judgement, then that consent should be treated in the same way as the consent of the patient himself in so far as civil liability is concerned. The attorney should have similar protection from civil liability where he is permitted to make decisions relating to the special types of procedures which are considered in Chapter 5.

> **Q53.** **What safeguards would be needed to ensure these recommendations would work in practice?**

The form of a CPA

6.16. The Law Commission recommended that, where a document purporting to be a CPA does not meet the statutory requirements, it should not be valid.

Acting in the donor's best interests

6.17. The Law Commission recommended that, although an attorney should not be under a general duty to act, where the attorney does act, he or she should be required to do so in the donor's best interests. This would be a principle which could be applied to all areas of decision-making which might be included, with the exception that if the attorney has been specifically authorised to consent to the discontinuation of artificial nutrition and hydration, procedures for the benefit of others and non-therapeutic research, they would need to have regard to the best interests guidance.

Statutory conditions and restrictions on a CPA

6.18. The main aspect of concern regarding a CPA is that it can be very wide and thus it may be difficult to ensure adequate safeguards. The Law Commission has dealt with some of these explicitly as follows.

6.19. The Law Commission recommended that the restriction against coercion and confinement should also apply to attorneys.

6.20. The Law Commission also proposed that no attorney should be able to consent to or refuse medical treatment while the patient has the capacity to make this decision. This would ensure that the dialogue between patient and doctor was not disturbed and complies with one of the Law Commission's other recommendations regarding health care, namely that a doctor should ensure that the patient is encouraged to participate in the decision-making process regarding his or her treatment as far as is possible.

6.21. The Law Commission also recommended that an attorney should not be able to consent to the donor's admission to hospital for assessment or treatment for mental disorder where such admission is against the will of the donor. This will go some way to reassure those with concerns that people with limited capacity may be confined against their will, for example where they are causing a nuisance in residential homes.

6.22. The Government accepts these recommendations.

6.23. The Law Commission recommended that an attorney should not be able to withhold basic care from the donor or refuse consent to its provision. A person with capacity would not be able to refuse such care by an advance statement either. As has been noted in paragraph 5.26, however, the Government has reservations about the possibility of force-feeding.

6.24. The Law Commission also recommended that an attorney should not be able to consent to treatment where the patient had made an advance refusal unless expressly authorised to do so.

6.25. The Government seeks further views on the proposal that attorneys should be able to refuse treatment on behalf of a patient where there is no explicit advance refusal. The best interests criteria outlined by the Law Commission include a requirement that regard should be had to the views of people whom it is appropriate and practicable to consult about the person's wishes and feelings and what would be in their best interests. This criterion would therefore ensure that the views of donees of a power of attorney are taken into account in almost every case. It might be that this is a more appropriate provision than to provide donees of a CPA with any further powers to refuse treatment. That said, the Government acknowledges that to prevent an attorney from refusing treatment on behalf of the donor would be a significant restriction on the powers proposed by the Law Commission.

6.26. The Law Commission recommended that, in cases where court approval or independent supervision of a decision would normally be required, the attorney should only be able to consent to treatment where expressly authorised to do so. This would also apply to discontinuation of artificial nutrition or hydration, procedures for the benefit of others and non-therapeutic research. In doing this the Law Commission were trying to strike a balance between the autonomy of the patient and ensuring that a controversial decision should not be made without proper consideration.

> **Q54.** **What safeguards would be needed to ensure that such a recommendation would work in practice?**

6.27. The Law Commission also suggested that an attorney would need to be expressly authorised to consider any refusal of treatment which might sustain life. Again this is a question which may be more appropriately covered by the best interests criteria.

THE DONOR AND THE DONEE
The donor

6.28. The Law Commission recommended that a donor of a CPA must be at least 18. This would ensure there was no overlap with the provisions of the Children Act 1989 or wardship. This, however, leaves the position of a competent near adult uncertain when, in the absence of an effective parental relationship, they may have good reason to want to nominate an adult to take health treatment decisions for them if they become incapacitated.

6.29. The Government acknowledges that the Law Commission's proposal would leave a young person for whom no one has parental responsibility in an anomalous situation. The Government would therefore welcome views on how this might be dealt with.

> **Q55.** **Should a person between the ages of 16 and 18 be permitted to be a donor?**

The donee

6.30. The Law Commission recommended that a donee might be the holder for the time being of a specified office. This was in response to representations made by the Public Trustee and the Association of Directors of Social Services among others, that a public official might occasionally be required to act as an attorney of last resort. This provision would ensure that, where a person was threatened with the loss of capacity, they would have someone to act on their behalf.

> **Q56.** **Would such a recommendation be workable in practice?**

CREATING, AMENDING, TERMINATING AND REGISTERING A CPA
Right to amend or terminate a CPA

6.31. The Law Commission recommended that a person should be able to amend or terminate their donation of a CPA at any time where they retained the capacity to do this. The Law Commission also recommended that a donor of a CPA should be able to appoint a person to replace the donee in the event of the donee: disclaiming the power of attorney, dying, becoming bankrupt (in relation to financial matters only), becoming incapacitated, or becoming divorced from the donor.

6.32. The Government accepts this recommendation.

Form of the CPA

6.33. The Law Commission recommended that, to ensure a donor and donee of a CPA understand the implications of this authority, the prescribed form of a CPA should include explanatory material. The donor would be required to state that he or she intends the power of attorney to continue in spite of supervening mental incapacity, and he or she would be required to state that they had read the explanatory information, or had it read to them. The Law Commission also recommend that the donee must state that he or she understands the duty to act in the donor's best interests.

6.34. The Government accepts this recommendation in principle, but will give further consideration to the form of such material, particularly for people who have reading difficulties or whose first language is not English. The views of respondents are welcomed.

> **Q57. What provision should be made for people who have reading difficulties or whose first language is not English?**

6.35. The Law Commission also recommended that the donee be required to state that they understand the principle of best interests which must inform their treatment of the donor when they lose capacity.

6.36. The Government accepts this recommendation in principle.

General power

6.37. The Law Commission have concluded that a CPA can confer a general power, as long as the explanatory material makes clear the nature of the power granted.

6.38. The great majority of EPAs currently submitted to the Court of Protection are general, in that they grant power in relation to all a donee's property and affairs. The Government would welcome views as to whether this general approach is considered appropriate for CPAs, or whether *specific* powers should be listed, which could provide an additional safeguard against abuse.

> **Q58. Should a CPA be able to grant general authority, or should specific matters be listed on the form?**[4]

---

4 *As recommended by the Law Commission in para. 7.13 of Consultation Paper 128.*

EXECUTION AND REGISTRATION REQUIREMENTS
Execution

6.39. The Law Commission's provisional proposal that a donor's capacity to execute should be subject to a certificate from a doctor and solicitor was regarded as overly intrusive by respondents to their consultation.

6.40. Although the Law Commission revised its view, and rejected a requirement for certification, the Government considers that a system for certification by a solicitor and a medical practitioner might help prevent unnecessary abuse of these powers.

> **Q59.** **Should there be a system for certification of CPAs by a solicitor and/or a medical practitioner?**

Registration

6.41. Respondents to the Law Commission's Consultation Paper were equally divided over whether a system of registration was necessary.

6.42. Registration has the advantage of bringing a document into the public domain and establishing its formal validity. It may also discourage some people from applying to register a CPA who might have abused the authority conferred by it. On the other hand, a purely administrative procedure may not provide adequate safeguards.

6.43. The Government would welcome suggestions for a system of registration that performs a clearly useful function; is simple and easily understood; and incorporates sufficient safeguards for donor and donee either through this or some other certification system. Experience with the registration of EPAs has shown that there is little advantage in having an administrative registration system which presents at best a hurdle and at worst a pitfall to honest attorneys, but can easily be evaded by those with fraudulent intentions. It may be that the only effective choice is between making powers of attorney inexpensive and easy to operate for the honest majority with the attendant risk, or deciding that the risk of abuse of a vulnerable minority cannot be tolerated and that formal controls should therefore be imposed on all for the protection of the minority. Views are sought upon whether it is necessary to choose between these two options and whether it is realistic to seek a workable compromise between them.

> **Q60.** **What safeguards should accompany a registration system for CPAs?**

6.44. The Government accepts the Law Commission's recommendation that no document should create a CPA unless it is in the prescribed form.

6.45. The Law Commission recommended that a registration authority should be appointed by the Lord Chancellor to register CPAs. The Law Commission envisaged that this function was likely to be undertaken by the Public Trust Office (PTO). The Government accepts that there is a strong case for the PTO taking on this work, but seeks views on whether this is generally considered acceptable.

> ***Q61.*** *Would the Public Trust Office be the most appropriate registering authority?*

> ***Q62.*** *What structure and function should the registering authority take?*

Notification

6.46. The donee is, under the Law Commission's proposed scheme, required to notify the donor that he or she intends to register the CPA. The CPA will not be registered if the donor objects (unless the court so orders). The Law Commission recommended that, once a CPA had been registered, formal notice should be given to the donor by the registration authority.

6.47. In relation to enduring powers of attorney this can be dispensed with – for example, where the donor is in a coma and the notification would thus serve little purpose. The Law Commission did not think this needed to be replicated because, under their new scheme, the registration of a CPA could be effected at any time and not only if the donor loses capacity.

6.48. The Law Commission also recommended that there should be notification to others once the CPA *had been* registered rather than *when there is an intention* to register. The people to be notified would be left to the donor but there would be a limit of two people.

6.49. The Government has a number of practical concerns about this proposal, on which views are sought:

> ***Q63.*** *What safeguards should be implemented to minimise the risk of fraudulent registration?*

> ***Q64.*** *What period of notice should be allowed between notification of registration and the ability to use the power of attorney?*

> ***Q65.*** *What proof of service of notification should be required before an attorney is authorised to act?*

MODIFICATION AND TERMINATION OF A CPA

6.50. There are two areas to balance here:

> the protection of the donor; and

> the protection of the donee where they are acting in good faith, believing that the CPA still applies.

Powers to modify or extend the scope of a CPA

6.51. The Law Commission recommended that the terms of a CPA should be capable of extension by the court where this is in the best interests of the donor, such as when new circumstances come to light in which decisions outside the scope of the CPA are needed and the court feels that the donee is best placed to deal with these.

6.52. Such decisions will only work where the donee is willing to take on this additional responsibility: they must be able to refuse. The donor will, however, be able to exclude this specifically in his or her CPA. This balances the right of the individual to make certain choices and the need to ensure that decisions can be taken in his or her best interests.

6.53. The Government accepts this recommendation in principle, and will give further consideration to the form of the explanatory material which would make this possibility clear to potential donors and donees.

Disclaimers

6.54. The Law Commission recommend that no disclaimer of a CPA should be valid unless the required notice is given to the donor and the registration authority.

6.55. The Government accepts this recommendation in principle, and will ensure that it is made clear to potential donees that this applies when they take on this responsibility.

Revoking a CPA

6.56. The Law Commission recommended that a donor of a CPA should have the power to revoke it at any time that they had the capacity to do so. In tandem with this they recommended that the provisions of section 5 of the 1971 Powers of Attorney Act should continue to apply so that a donee acting on the authority of the CPA is protected from liability as long as they do not know of the revocation.

6.57. The Government accepts this recommendation.

Divorce and bankruptcy

6.58. The Law Commission suggested a number of specific provisions to deal with the bankruptcy of a donee or the divorce of donor and donee.

6.59. Although it is perfectly understandable that a person who is bankrupt should not be able to deal with the financial or property affairs of a donor, the Law Commission saw no reason why this should apply to personal welfare or health care decisions.

6.60. Unless the donor has specifically instructed to the contrary, the Law Commission also thought that the dissolution or annulment of a donor and donee's marriage should denote the end of a CPA, just as it noted the end of their relationship. This does not preclude the donor from deciding that his or her former partner is the person they would wish to make these decisions. A reminder notice will need to be placed on the decree absolute (or the divorce order once Part II of the Family Law Act 1996 comes into force).

6.61. The Government accepts these recommendations.

Limitations on the powers of the registration authority

6.62. The Law Commission limited the registration authority's powers to cancelling the registration of a CPA on the basis of:

a revocation by the donor;

a disclaimer by the donee;

the death of the donee;

the expiry of the time limit;

the donee becoming incapacitated;

the divorce or annulment of the marriage of donor and donee; or

evidence of the bankruptcy or winding up of the donee.

6.63. The registration authority should also be required to attach an appropriate notice on the CPA to note any changes.

6.64. The functions envisaged are thus purely administrative. Views are sought on whether this is considered appropriate, and in particular, on whether there are any circumstances in which an administrative registration authority should refuse to register a CPA. (For example, must it accept a CPA which appears on its face to be a forgery or it is so materially defective that there is doubt about whether it is properly a CPA at all?) Any power to reject requires the exercise of a discretion.

Q66. **Should the functions of the registering authority be administrative only?**

POWERS OF THE COURT
Powers of the court

6.65. The Law Commission made a distinction between the administrative powers of the registration authority and the judicial functions of the court. The powers of the court will include:

determining the meaning or effect of a CPA;

determining whether a donor has the capacity to create or revoke a CPA;

determining whether revocation has been effective;

giving directions to the donee where the donor loses capacity, including directions as to the production of information, reports, accounts and records;

determining a donee's remuneration and expenses;

relieving an attorney from some or all of the liability arising from a breach of duty; and

the power to direct that a power of attorney should not be registered, or should be revoked if it has been registered where fraud or undue influence was used to create it.

6.66. The above powers reflect the existing jurisdiction in relation to EPAs. In addition, the Law Commission recommended that the Court of Protection should also gain new powers, for example to cure defects in a CPA, where the intention was clearly to create a CPA.

6.67. The Government accepts this recommendation in principle, as long as it is clear to what extent the court can consider a CPA. There should not, for example, be any question of a CPA being granted where the donor lacked capacity or where the donor and donee had not been given the opportunity to consider the relevant explanatory information and so did not fully understand the implications of their actions.

Q67. Under what circumstances should the court not be able to cure defects in a CPA?

6.68. The Law Commission recommended that the court should have the power to appoint an attorney, where the donee was no longer able or willing to act. This would be judicial intervention of last resort as a donor already has the opportunity, under the Law Commission proposals, to appoint a substitute donee in the event of this happening. This would therefore only be available in cases where the donor had lost the capacity to act. The Law Commission were not prepared to extend this to those cases where no CPA had been made, on the grounds that the person had not contemplated giving decision-making authority to another person.

6.69. The Law Commission also recommended that the court should be able to direct either that a purported CPA should not be registered or revoke a CPA where the donee or intended donee has behaved, is behaving or proposes to behave in a way that either contravenes or would contravene the authority granted in the CPA, or is not or would not be in the donor's best interests.

6.70. The Government accepts these recommendations.

Transitionals

6.71. The Law Commission recommended that no EPA should be able to be made after any proposals on CPAs are brought into force. Transitional provisions will be needed for some EPAs made prior to the repeal of the 1985 Act.

6.72. The Government accepts this recommendation.

Option to convert

6.73. The Law Commission would prefer that, if a person wishes to make a CPA, they should destroy any existing EPA. They have, however, suggested that a person should be able to convert an EPA into a CPA. These conversions would have the same conditions as the making of an entirely new CPA, i.e. the donor would need to be capable of the decision, both donor and donee would need to have read and understood the explanatory materials provided, and the usual registration procedures would apply. The form for such a conversion would be prescribed. The Government believes that this is likely to cause an increase in workload for the PTO if they become the registration authority. In addition, an option to convert would almost certainly prove more bureaucratic and confusing than simply creating a new CPA from scratch. The Government would welcome views.

Q68.   Is there a need for an option to convert an EPA into a CPA?

MISCELLANEOUS

6.74. The Law Commission considered that innocent attorneys and third parties should have some protection where they rely on an invalidly registered CPA. This is similar to the protection currently afforded to third parties who rely on an invalid EPA.

6.75. The Government accepts this recommendation.

Decision-Making by the Court

BACKGROUND

7.1. The Law Commission recommended, in support of their proposals for a unified system of decision-making to cover financial, personal welfare and health care matters, that there should also be a court jurisdiction which could deal with all of these areas together. This proposal was supported overwhelmingly on consultation. The Law Commission wanted the jurisdiction to balance the principle of the autonomy of the individual with the need to ensure adequate protection for the person concerned. The Law Commission did, however, view the court as being principally the option of last resort in cases of dispute.

7.2. The Court of Protection and the Public Trust Office (PTO) currently deal only with financial matters, although in some cases there will be issues of personal welfare, for example in terms of how money is spent to provide the best possible care. The Law Commission's proposals would thus require a major extension to these organisations' jurisdiction with implications not only for resourcing in general but specifically for the basis on which the PTO is currently funded. Details of the operation of the PTO, the Court of Protection and the Official Solicitor are attached at Annex D.

A UNIFIED JURISDICTION

7.3. The Government sees merit in a unified jurisdiction, but there would clearly be practical implications for the court system and the PTO. The Government will take forward consideration of how best to implement these recommendations, if respondents consider this to be the most appropriate way forward.

> **Q69.** **Should there be a single court jurisdiction, able to deal with all areas of decision-making (financial, welfare, and health care)?**

> **Q70.** **Does the current Court of Protection offer the most appropriate base for such a jurisdiction?**

ROLE OF THE COURT

7.4. The Law Commission identified three types of determination which a court might be asked to make:

a declaration;

an order; or

an order appointing a manager.

7.5. The two principles which the court would need to bear in mind are:

the nature and extent of the decision-making capacity of the person concerned; and

the principle that, in general, any decision taken must be in that person's best interests[1].

7.6. The Law Commission recommended, as part of the best interests criteria, that the least restrictive option should always be chosen. They thought it was thus unnecessary to include a "no order" principle in their draft Bill. The "no order" principle contained in the Children Act 1989 states that the court should not make an order unless it is satisfied that making an order would be better for the child than not doing so.

7.7. The Government accepts the principle that, whenever decisions of this nature are taken, and in whatever forum, the least restrictive option should always be chosen, but would welcome views as to whether there is a need for a "no order" principle.

Q71. Should legislation in this area include a "no order" principle?

7.8. The Law Commission thought that the inherent jurisdiction of the court to make declarations as to the lawfulness of a particular course of action where remedies are not provided under any statutory scheme would remain as a safeguard, although it envisaged that most decisions required in this area would now fall within the new statutory jurisdiction.

Declarations

7.9. The Law Commission thought that the court should have the power to make declarations as to the question of the capacity of a person or the validity or applicability of an advance refusal of treatment, where this was either in dispute or where there was uncertainty.

7.10. The Government accepts this recommendation in principle and seeks views as to whether such a declaratory power should apply to other types of advance statements and delegated decision-making, such as powers of attorney.

Q72a. Should any decision-making forum have the power to declare:

    i.   whether or not a person has capacity; or

    ii.   whether or not an advance statement is valid; or

    iii.   whether or not authority (such as a CPA) should be delegated?

---

1   *Possible exceptions to this principle are discussed in paragraphs 5.23 – 5.29.*

> **Q72b.** *If so, how should such a declaration cater for the needs of those with fluctuating conditions, such as manic depression, where the person concerned may have unpredictable periods of complete lucidity when substitute decision-making is not required?*

Orders and appointments

7.11. At present, where the property in question does not exceed £5,000, or where it is "otherwise appropriate", the Court of Protection will make a short order rather than appoint a receiver. The Law Commission suggested that this limit should be removed so that the court was given full discretion depending on the circumstances of the case. They suggested that short orders should be used wherever possible as this would limit the amount of intervention in the life of the person without, or with limited, capacity.

7.12. The Law Commission recommended that the court's powers should be expressed as a broad, but non-exhaustive list to cover all those decisions on which an order might be necessary. They thus recommended that a court should be able to:

> make any decision on behalf of a person who lacks capacity to make that decision;

> appoint a manager[2] to be responsible for making a decision on behalf of such a person; and that these decisions could be in relation to any matter relating to the personal welfare, health care, property or affairs of the person concerned, including the conduct of legal proceedings.

> **Q73.** *Should the court be able to appoint a manager?*

> **Q74.** *If so, what should be the scope of a manager's responsibilities?*

> **Q75.** *What criteria should be used to decide who should be a manager?*

7.13. The Law Commission also recommended that the court have full flexibility as to the directions and orders necessary to give effect to their decisions and that the usual enforcement powers should apply. The Law Commission suggested that a decision of the court should be preferable to the appointment of a manager to make the jurisdiction as little interventionist as possible.

7.14. The Law Commission also recommended, in tandem with this proposal, that any appointment of a manager should be as limited as possible both in scope and duration.

7.15. The Law Commission recommended that the court should be able to make orders of its own motion where this is in the best interests of the person concerned, regardless of the terms of the application made to the court.

7.16. The Government sees merit in these recommendations, and recognises that it is unlikely that any restrictions on the stage at which the court would become involved would be helpful as urgent decisions or disputes may occur at any time. However, the Government would not wish to increase the powers of the court to such an extent without prior consultation.

---

2. *The Law Commission envisaged that the court would be most likely to appoint as manager a family member or other carer. A manager's role would therefore be similar to that of attorney, although a manager's remit (as befits a decision-maker who is not appointed by the person him or herself) would be more restricted than that of an attorney*

Q76. *Are there any circumstances in which the discretion of the court in these areas should be limited?*

PERSONAL WELFARE

7.17. The Law Commission recommended that a number of issues should only be able to be decided by the person themselves, namely:

consent to marriage

consent to sexual relations

agreement to divorce on the basis of two years separation with consent (*this will be rendered redundant by the implementation of Part II of the Family Law Act 1996*)

voting at an election for any public office

consent to adoption or to the freeing of a child for adoption

the discharge of parental responsibility, except in relation to a child's property

7.18. The Law Commission stressed that the court should have no powers to make decisions which the person without capacity could not have made, even if they had retained their capacity. The court could not, for example, refuse basic care.

7.19. The Law Commission's draft Bill makes explicit reference to the court's power to determine where a person should live and with whom they should have contact. The Law Commission recommended that the provision regarding residence should not include the power to order detention in hospital which would be subject to provisions in the Mental Health Act. The Children Act 1989 also has explicit provisions for a specific issue order, which can decide nearly any personal welfare issue regarding a child which may arise, and a prohibited steps order, which can prevent action being taken where this is regarded as not in the child's best interests. There are also provisions which prevent the child being removed from the jurisdiction.

7.20. The Government accepts in principle the Law Commission's recommendations relating to personal welfare decision-making by the court, but seeks views on whether explicit provision is desirable for other orders as well as residence or contact orders. It would not be appropriate to equate the provisions for adults without capacity with those for children, but it is necessary to ensure that issues such as the educational or other needs of the person without capacity can be adequately handled.

Q77. *Should explicit provision be made for the court to make other orders in addition to residence and contact orders?*

7.21. The Law Commission thought it was necessary to ensure that non-molestation orders could be made to protect the person without capacity and also orders preventing an individual from having contact with a person without capacity. It may be possible for some people without capacity to be protected by the provisions of Part IV of the Family Law Act 1996, which came into force on 1 October 1997, or by the Protection from Harassment Act 1997 which creates a new criminal offence for a person who pursues a course of conduct which they know, or ought to have known, causes another to fear that an act of violence will be used against them. To ensure the widest possible protection, however, particularly from abuse by people outside the immediate family or household, the Law Commission thought a specific provision was necessary. The Law Commission recommended that this provision should extend only to protection and should not impinge on the rights of others, such as the right to occupy a home. This would principally be covered by other remedies such as those in the Family Law Act or other property legislation.

7.22. The Government accepts this recommendation.

7.23. The Law Commission also recommended that the court's powers should cover the exercise of a person's statutory rights to information, and that the court should be able to apply for or obtain benefits and services for the person concerned. This would ensure that where relatives or carers for a person without capacity have difficulties in being recognised by local authorities or other service providers, the court can give such people the back up required to ensure the person without capacity is granted their full entitlement.

7.24. The Government accepts these recommendations in principle.

HEALTH CARE

7.25. The Law Commission recommended that the court's powers in this area should extend to:

approving or refusing approval for particular forms of health care;

appointing a manager to consent or refuse consent to particular forms of health care;

requiring a person to allow a different person to take over the health care of a patient; and

obtaining access to health care records.

7.26. The Government is concerned about the element of this recommendation which would enable a court-appointed manager to refuse health care. A court-appointed manager might have less prior knowledge of a patient's wishes regarding treatment than the patient's doctor. The Government therefore seeks views on this element of the recommendation.

> **Q78.** *Should a court-appointed manager have the power to refuse consent to particular forms of health care?*

7.27. The Law Commission recommended that the court or a court-appointed manager should not be able to:

refuse basic care; or

consent to treatment which has been covered by an advance refusal.

7.28. The Government accepts this recommendation in principle.

Non-therapeutic research procedures

7.29. The Law Commission recommended that any authority for a manager to consent to non-therapeutic research should be specifically granted by the court. This reflects the rest of the Law Commission's Report which suggests that such a decision requires special safeguards.

7.30. The Government is also concerned about a manager's likely lack of medical expertise or prior knowledge of the patient's wishes in this area, and would welcome views on whether a manager should be able to consent to non-therapeutic research procedures.

Q79.   Should a manager be able to consent to non-therapeutic research procedures?

Admission to hospital as if under the Mental Health Act 1983

7.31. The Law Commission recommended that the court should only have the power to order admission to hospital for assessment or treatment if they are satisfied, on the evidence of two doctors (one of whom at least should be approved for the purposes of section 12 of the Mental Health Act 1983), that the grounds for admission set out in sections 2 or 3 respectively of the Mental Health Act 1983 exist and it is appropriate, having regard to the best interests criteria, that the person concerned should be admitted to hospital.

7.32. The Law Commission also recommended that anyone admitted to hospital under such a procedure should not be able to apply to the Mental Health Review Tribunal in their first period in hospital, as admission would be a result of a judicial determination.

7.33. The Government seeks views about these recommendations. In particular, if a person meets the criteria for compulsory admission to hospital under the Mental Health Act 1983, should they rather be admitted under the existing provisions? Would there be a risk of confusion if a new procedure with the same purpose were to be introduced?

Q80.   Is there a need for a new provision for compulsory admission to hospital?

PROPERTY AND AFFAIRS

7.34. The Law Commission recommended, in response to a point made by the Master of the Court of Protection, that the Court should be able to exercise its jurisdiction with regard to property and affairs in respect of a child under 16, if it is clear that the lack of capacity is likely to last into adulthood. The Court of Protection currently has no lower age limit on its jurisdiction and the Master believes that it is sometimes in the child's best interests to make financial orders as soon as possible e.g. where an award for a large amount of money has been made and the child is unlikely ever to be able to have the capacity to make decisions in relation to this sum.

7.35. The Law Commission produced a list of those decisions in relation to property and affairs regarding which the court should be able to make an order. The criteria to be considered would be what was in the best interests of the person concerned. This would enable issues such as gifts to be included. The court could also appoint a manager to deal with any of the issues listed. These are the:

control and management of any property;

disposal of any property;

acquisition of any property;

carrying on of a business, trade or profession;

dissolution of any partnership;

carrying out of any contract; and

discharge of any debt or obligation.

7.36. The Government accepts these recommendations.

7.37. The Law Commission recommended that some financial decisions should be retained by the court and should not be delegated to court-appointed managers. One of these would be the power to set up a trust for the person concerned. The Court of Protection rarely uses such provisions at present, but consultees thought these powers should at least be available. The Law Commission subsequently thought that only the court should have powers regarding:

making a settlement of any property, whether with the person concerned or with others as beneficiary or beneficiaries;

making a will; and

exercising powers vested in the person concerned.

7.38. The Government accepts this recommendation in principle. Further consideration will need to be given as to whether this should also include the conduct of legal proceedings.

7.39. The Law Commission also discussed the current procedures of the Court of Protection. They noted that at present most cases involve the appointment of the Public Trust Office (PTO) as financial manager. The Law Commission thought it might be appropriate for a wider range of bodies to be appointed e.g. solicitors, accountants, investment managers etc, especially against the background of the fees charged by the PTO. Such individuals would be required to give security and submit regular reports and accounts to the Public Trustee.

7.40. The Law Commission thought that an expansion of private appointees in this area might also be valuable given that the PTO does not have a regional presence at present. No legislative change would be required here, it would be one of practice.

7.41. There are, however, a number of possible drawbacks to implementing this proposal on a wide scale. First, although the Law Commission recommended that security should always be taken from financial managers, it is not clear that affordable security would necessarily be readily available to individuals who undertook sole responsibility for the management of substantial amounts of capital. Security is currently available to receivers at a modest cost to the patient because, with access to capital restricted by the Court or the PTO, the amount of money passing through their hands within any accounting period is limited. The additional risk in releasing large sums of capital without security, or the expense of security, might present an obstacle. In some cases, professional managers would be covered by indemnity insurance and the availability of this might, of necessity, result in professional managers being preferred over family members for financial reasons, contrary to the Court's general practice at present. It could be seen as unfortunate for family members who are currently acting as receiver to be left without a formal role. Although the PTO does charge fees, so would professional managers and it is not clear that the latter would be less expensive when the fact that the PTO is non-profit making and is able to offer economies of scale are taken into account. In any event some fees would have to be charged by the PTO to finance its more limited supervisory role. Also, although solicitors' costs can be taxed, there are no formal mechanisms for the control of costs charged by other professionals such as accountants and investment managers. On balance, it would seem sensible for the Court of Protection to retain as wide a discretion to deal with each case in the way which seems most appropriate on its particular facts, without any presumption in favour of, or against, private appointees.

MANAGERS APPOINTED BY THE COURT

7.42. The Law Commission recommended that a manager should be a person of at least 18 years of age, or, in relation to financial matters only, a trust corporation. Although the Law Commission are of the view that the most appropriate candidates for appointment as managers would be those who already care for the person without capacity (or a friend or relative), they recommended that the holder of a specified office might be appointed as long as there was no conflict of interest.

7.43. The Government agrees these recommendations, and the underlying assumption that the court should be left with the widest possible choice of manager, subject to consultation about the possible role of managers of residential care establishments: see paragraphs 7.61 to 7.65, below.

Joint appointments

7.44. The Law Commission recommended that more than one manager might be appointed either to act jointly, successively or as a standby. This might be helpful particularly where the person is old or where a manager may need some expert assistance in some areas, such as from a social worker.

Duties and powers of managers

7.45. In general, a manager would have to act in the best interests of the person without capacity. The Government has sought views on whether a manager should be able to consent to non-therapeutic research procedures at paragraph 7.30, above. Were a manager able to consent to such procedures they would need to have regard to the best interests checklist.

7.46. A manager who failed to act at all when a decision within the scope of his or her duties was needed would be in breach of his or her duty. This position would differ from that of attorneys, who are not under a duty to act. The Law Commission thus recommended that the court should be able to vary or discharge an order appointing a manager who fails to fulfil this obligation.

7.47. The Law Commission favoured an express provision to determine the status of someone acting as a manager. At present a receiver of the kind appointed by the Court of Protection is a statutory agent of the patient. The property of the person without capacity is not vested in the receiver and the receiver is not personally liable for the costs of anyone he or she employs. The Law Commission proposed that this position should apply to court appointed managers under the new jurisdiction. They also proposed that any guidance issued to managers would recommend that they should always notify any third party that they were acting as a manager for a person without capacity.

7.48. The Law Commission recommended that no manager should be able to make a decision which is inconsistent with a decision by a donee of a CPA acting within his or her authority. This gives clear precedence to someone acting in accord with the person without capacity's express wishes. If a manager is dissatisfied or is concerned that such a decision is not in the person without capacity's best interests, he or she can apply to the court.

7.49. The court manager will incur civil liability where he breaches his duties as a manager and acts outside the scope of his authority. The Government considers that where a manager consents to medical treatment which health care providers consider should be given to the patient in accordance with their clinical judgement, then that consent should be treated in the same way as the consent of the patient himself in so far as civil liability is concerned.

7.50. The Government accepts these recommendations.

Time limits for appointment

7.51. Currently, there are no time limits on the appointment of receivers or the designation of a person as a patient of the Court of Protection. Under the Law Commission's proposals the Court of Protection would be obliged to make an order or appointment for the shortest time duration deemed to be necessary. The maximum time limit of five years for an appointment suggested by the Law Commission would provide for regular review, which currently does not occur. It would thus provide a safeguard for what is a wide power. This recommendation would have resource implications for the Court and the PTO, as they do not currently have this automatic review function.

7.52. However, there are a number of practical drawbacks to this proposal. The sad reality is that for the vast majority of the patients of the Court of Protection, there is no possibility of recovering capacity and many will die within five years of the receivership order being made. In the majority of cases, setting up and operating a procedure whereby an appointment expired and had to be reviewed by the court after a fixed period, would achieve nothing and could prove to be a waste of resources. If there were 40,000 cases subject to the jurisdiction of the Court, this would mean, on a five year cycle, that 8,000 had to be reviewed each year, with serious implications for the workload of the Court of Protection and PTO and consequent additional cost to the patient. The expiry of an appointment could also cause serious difficulties in a minority of cases where, for whatever reason, the date of expiry was overlooked, and occurred, for example, right in the middle of a conveyancing transaction. The manager would then have acted without authority and the transaction would be invalid. A lot of time and trouble might be incurred in remedying the situation. If the concern is to provide a safeguard for a wide power, it might be more effective to make permanent orders in most cases, but to identify cases where there is a genuine possibility of recovery and restrict any review system to these.

> **Q81.** **Is there a need for time limited appointments in the majority of cases, or the disadvantages of this in terms of expense and possible inconvenience outweigh any likely advantages?**

Protection for the person concerned

7.53. The Law Commission recommended that managers should continue to be asked for security and should be asked for accounts on a yearly basis as is currently the case. In some cases there will be no authority to deal with financial matters, but the Law Commission thought that reports would still be required. Although the Public Trust Office deal with security and annual accounts at present, they have no experience in personal welfare or health matters. There would thus be resource implications in terms of workload and training and also for the policy of the PTO covering its costs. Although some patients in respect of whom the Court of Protection was asked to exercise its new health and welfare jurisdiction would have means and be able to meet the costs from their own resources, it is likely that many would not.

> **Q82.** **Would these recommendations work in practice?**

Monitoring by the Public Trustee

7.54. A majority of respondents to consultation supported the need for a monitoring function. The Law Commission thought that this should lie with the PTO as:

> they already had experience of financial matters, many of which were related to personal welfare; and

> there should be one place which monitored all decisions: they should not be split into health, financial, and personal welfare.

> **Q83.** **Are these recommendations workable in practice?**

7.55. Under the Law Commission's scheme, the Public Trustee would be an administrator, with all judicial matters falling to the Court of Protection.

7.56. The Public Trustee's role would involve:

> appointment as manager (as at present);

> receiving security and accounts (as at present); and

> monitoring other managers (this will be an extension e.g. the health and personal welfare jurisdiction).

7.57. The Law Commission recommended that the Public Trustee's powers in this regard be set out in Rules. These powers would include:

raising questions on managers' reports;

directing a Lord Chancellor's Visitor to visit and report on whether the Public Trustee should exercise any of his or her functions; and

inspecting property or directing an appropriate person to do so.

Q84. *Would the recommendations relating to the supervisory role of the Public Trustee work in practice?*

Expenses and remuneration for the manager

7.58. The Law Commission did not recommend any change to the current position whereby the court can direct whether remuneration should be paid from the estate. The difficulty here will be managing welfare and health decisions where the person without capacity has no money. This has implications for the entire funding structure of the PTO and it is questionable whether other organisations are likely to wish to get involved with such functions. The Law Commission also recommended that the Public Trustee should be able to charge a fee for the supervisory functions envisaged. Currently the Public Trustee experiences problems in providing resources to meet the needs of those persons for whom she acts as receiver. A receiver's powers and duties relate only to financial issues but in practice, it is difficult to separate financial from welfare issues where patients have little alternative but to rely upon the PTO to decide on such issues. The current work of the PTO is therefore necessarily labour intensive and costly.

7.59. The Government accepts this recommendation in principle, subject to respondents' views about whether this proposal would offer protection for those with no resources, and will give further consideration to the implications for the Public Trust Office.

Q85. *How would the recommendation that managers be remunerated operate where the incapacitated adult has no finances? In particular, what funding mechanism should be put in place?*

Code of practice

7.60. The Law Commission recommended that the Secretary of State issue a Code of Practice to managers. The Government would welcome views on the desirability and content of such a Code.

Q86. *Is there a need for a Code of Practice in this area, and, if so, what should be included in such a code?*

MANAGEMENT OF RESIDENTS' FUNDS BY CARE ESTABLISHMENTS

7.61. The question of care establishments managing the funds of incapable residents was considered by the Scottish Law Commission, and was the subject of further consultation by the Scottish Office.

7.62. Where a resident of a residential care home or nursing home has capacity but is unable or unwilling to manage his or her own financial affairs, the resident may give instructions to a care home manager to act as agent. Where a resident is in receipt of social security benefits, the Secretary of State can appoint the care home manager to make benefit claims on that person's behalf and to deal with the benefits paid. However, Government guidance for both these circumstances states that care home managers should be given such responsibilities where no one else (for example, a relative) is able to take them on. The Government believes that the same principles should apply in the case of an incapable adult.

7.63. There are inevitable difficulties in this area: as with any attorney or court-appointed manager, care home managers may find themselves in situations where there is a conflict of interest inherent in the management of a patient's financial affairs as well as their personal welfare and health care. These tensions would be exacerbated in the case of residential care homes, as a patient's financial status is inextricably linked with that of the home itself. The Government believes that, because of the difficulties in this area, there should be a general assumption against care home managers being appointed as managers of incapable residents' funds. In those cases where no one else is able to take on the responsibilities of manager, the local authority should normally take on the role.

7.64. In exceptional circumstances, a care home manager might be felt to be the most appropriate person to be appointed as manager, but in those cases, tight controls would be needed. Funds held on behalf of residents would have to be kept separate from those of the establishment, and the establishment would need to keep separate records of how those funds were spent. It would be necessary for the care home manager to be specifically approved, and his or her transactions on behalf of residents monitored.

7.65. It might make sense for this approval and monitoring to be the responsibility of local authorities and health authorities, who already register and inspect residential care homes and nursing homes respectively. Managers would be required to keep records of all their transactions on behalf of residents, and local authority and health authority inspectors would have the power to inspect those records at any time. In addition, managers would be required to submit annual accounts of all their transactions on behalf of residents for sample audit by the Public Trustee.

> **Q87a.** *Should there be a general assumption that care home managers should not be appointed as managers of an incapable adult's financial affairs?*

> **Q87b.** *Are there circumstances in which, despite the conflict of interest, a care home manager might be the most suitable person?*

> **Q88.** *If care home managers are to be allowed to carry out this role, what approval and monitoring systems should there be?*

chapter

Public Law Protection for People at Risk

BACKGROUND

8.1. The Law Commission's main aim in this area was to make provisions to ensure that people without capacity, and other vulnerable adults, constituting a broader group of people who may not be able to protect themselves from harm, were protected from abuse and neglect. They regarded the existing powers as draconian and thought that this resulted in the powers being inadequately used.

8.2. The recommendations of the Law Commission Report are consistent with the community care system. They also attempt to balance the need to ensure adequate protection is available to vulnerable people with the need to be sensitive to the needs of carers and those without capacity, who might both want and be able to take responsibility for some decisions concerning their welfare.

8.3. The Law Commission thus recommended that:

social services authorities should have a new duty to investigate cases of possible neglect or abuse; and

they should have short term powers to deal with the protection of people they believe to be at risk, including powers to deal with those who attempt to obstruct them in their exercise of this duty.

8.4. The proposals met with a positive response on consultation, but some carers' groups were concerned, wanting greater focus on access to services rather than enforcement procedures. The former is outside the scope of these proposals.

8.5. Under the Registered Homes Act 1984, local authorities and health authorities have powers of inspection, investigation and enforcement in relation to residential care homes and nursing homes respectively. While there is no reason to exclude care home residents from the duty proposed for local authorities, in practice it is expected that where there is suspicion of abuse in a care home, the most appropriate course of action will be through the Registered Homes Act powers rather than powers discussed in this chapter. It is important that all residents of the care home should be protected, not just the individual who may have suffered abuse.

8.6. The Government considers that there may be merit in some of the recommendations made in this area, but is not convinced that there is a pressing need for reform. Whilst it is important to protect vulnerable adults, the Government also believes that regard should be had to the rights of individuals to live in isolation if they so chose, even if at some degree of risk to themselves. The question of fitness to object could also be very difficult to judge. A number of initiatives have been undertaken to address the particular problem of elder abuse, and these cannot yet be fully evaluated. In the light of these concerns, the Government would particularly welcome views from local authorities, carers and mental health and learning disability organisations, on whether there is a need for legislation along the lines recommended by the Law Commission. If it is felt that such legislation is necessary, views would be welcomed on the practicalities of the proposals.

Q89. *Is there a need for legislation in this area?*

DEFINING THE CLIENT GROUP

8.7. The Law Commission have suggested a broad definition of a vulnerable person, as someone of 16 years or over who:

> is or may be in need of community care services by reason of mental or other disability, age or illness; and who

> is or may be unable to take care of him or herself, or unable to protect him or herself against significant harm or exploitation.

8.8. The Law Commission did, however, stress that these powers should not be used to invade the rights of competent people. They envisaged the powers being necessary as a last resort and, more particularly, where another person was attempting to obstruct social services authorities attempts to undertake an assessment or provide care.

Children

8.9. The Law Commission recommended that children under 16 be excluded because they would be covered by the emergency provisions of the Children Act 1989. There will be some overlap with the Children Act provisions for young people of 16 and 17, and also (potentially) with the wardship jurisdiction. The Law Commission acknowledged this by including relevant services under the Children Act within their definition of community care services.

8.10. The views of respondents would be welcomed.

The meaning of "harm"

8.11. The Law Commission built on the significant harm test included in the Children Act in defining this term. They suggested that "harm" should be taken to include not only ill-treatment (including sexual abuse and forms of ill-treatment which are not physical), but also "the impairment of, or an avoidable deterioration in, physical or mental health, and the impairment of physical, intellectual, emotional, social or behavioural development". These latter categories may be very important to an individual's ability to recover from an illness or have the best possible quality of life. It is thus very much a provision to protect the general well-being and development of the vulnerable person.

8.12. The Government is minded to accept the principle of the recommendations relating to the meaning of harm, but would welcome views on the Law Commission's proposed definition of harm.

> **Q90.** **Is the proposed definition of harm appropriate?**

A DUTY TO INVESTIGATE

8.13. The Law Commission recommended the strengthening of existing provisions by introducing a duty on social services authorities to make enquiries where they have reason to believe that a vulnerable person in their area is suffering or likely to suffer significant harm or serious exploitation. This enquiry would be to determine whether this person is suffering or is likely to suffer such harm or exploitation and, if so, whether services should be provided or action taken to protect the person concerned. The Law Commission have restricted such powers to when a vulnerable person is at risk and not a more general duty.

8.14. Respondents to the Law Commission's consultation exercise asked for a specific reference to "exploitation" to be included in the proposals. This is already an issue in financial matters and might also occur in personal welfare or health matters, for example where a carer chooses not to provide the care needed on grounds of cost or some other motive. The Court of Protection report that exploitation does occur and it is thus likely that such safeguards will be required.

8.15. The Law Commission recommended that only social services authorities should have this duty. They feared that to extend this responsibility might lead to people falling between two stools, with authorities each believing the other intended to act.

8.16. The Government seeks views on the practical implications of this proposal. It is likely that this function is already in practice carried out by social services authorities and that it is appropriate for them to have the power to undertake such investigations.

> **Q91.** **Should social services authorities be required to investigate allegations of abuse or neglect of an incapacitated, mentally disordered or vulnerable adult?**
>
> **Q92.** **Should any other organisations, such as the police, hospital managers, or the trustees of charities, be given a similar power?**

8.17. The Law Commission also recommended that the local authority should be able to have access to information from a variety of statutory bodies[1] which might help them in their enquiries including in other regions.

8.18. The views of respondents on this would be welcomed.

---

1 Those listed in clause 37(5) of the Law Commission's draft Bill are (a) any local authority; (b) any local education authority; (c) any local housing authority; (d) any health authority; and (e) any person authorised by the Secretary of State for the purposes of this section.

Authorised officers

8.19. The Law Commission recommended that social services authorities should authorise certain officers to undertake such work.

> **Q93.** *Is it appropriate or practical for social services authorities (or any other organisation that it is thought should conduct investigations) to nominate authorised officers?*

EMERGENCY INTERVENTION

8.20. The Law Commission recommended a step-by-step approach to the exercise of such powers. These might need to be telescoped in an emergency.

8.21. The first of these steps would enable a local authority to gain access to premises where they believe a person at risk is living. This would extend only to reasonable times of the day and would include authority to inspect the premises concerned and interview the person believed to be at risk in private. The only restriction on this would be where the person concerned is believed to object, unless there is a question as to their suffering from a mental disability. The Law Commission's view was that officers should be obliged to give proof of their status.

Entry warrants

8.22. If an authorised officer is prevented from undertaking this duty, the Law Commission recommended that they should be able to apply for a warrant authorising a constable, accompanied by the authorised officer, to enter. Again, the local authority must believe the person to be at risk and they should not apply where they have reason to believe that the person concerned has the capacity and wish to reject this intervention. A warrant should be sought only if it is necessary to enable this investigation to be carried out. The proposal is similar to the power to issue search warrants under section 102 of the Children Act 1989.

8.23. The Law Commission recommended that any removal of the person at risk from the premises in question should only occur after an investigation had been completed.

8.24. The Government considers that there might be a case for telescoping the-step-by step nature of these provisions where the person is in imminent danger of significant harm if he or she is not removed from their place of residence immediately and does not object to such a removal.

> **Q94a.** *Should there be provision for telescoping these procedures in certain circumstances?*
>
> **Q94b.** *How might such telescoping work?*

Assessment orders

8.25. Where a person is believed to be at risk and is not believed to object or be capable of a reasoned objection, the Law Commission recommended that a local authority should be able to apply for an order for an assessment of this person where they are not otherwise able to do so. This equates to similar provision for child assessment orders under the Children Act 1989. As this provision is designed purely to allow assessment to take place in the short term, the Law Commission recommended that such orders should be time limited to a period of eight days. Some respondents argued that this period should be capable of extension to ensure that the assessment could be carried out. The Law Commission rejected this as the eight days would commence from the date specified in the assessment order, not the date the order was actually made. The Law Commission were also concerned to make the intervention as limited as possible.

8.26. The Government accepts the principle of this recommendation, subject to the following question:

> **Q95.** **Are there any circumstances in which the period of eight days should be extended?**

Medical assessment

8.27. The Law Commission recommended that any medical examination should be subject to the usual provisions, namely that the patient would have to consent to treatment unless there was a specific order of the court dispensing with such consent. In deciding to make such a ruling, the court would need to consider the patient's capacity to consent or refuse such an examination and whether it is in their best interest. It is suggested that the local authority would need to specify the details of the components of the assessment planned when applying for the court order as they are currently required to do under the Children Act 1989.

Removal from home

8.28. The Law Commission recommended that the removal of the vulnerable person from home in order to undertake an assessment should require the specific authorisation of the court.

8.29. The Government accepts these recommendations in principle, but would welcome views on the likely practical implications of the removal of the vulnerable person from the home. For instance, consideration will need to be given as to who should be notified of the removal, and how bills etc would be paid.

> **Q96.** **How would removal from the home work in practice?**

Temporary Protection Orders

8.30. The Law Commission recommended that the court be given the power to make temporary protection orders. While these may broadly equate with emergency protection orders under the Children Act, the Law Commission were keen to introduce a different term to take account of the sensitivities of those who might regard using the same wording as "infantilising" vulnerable adults. Such an order would only be made where a vulnerable person is at risk if they are not removed to or kept in protective accommodation, and where the applicant does not know or believe that the person objects to the order. Again there would be the question of whether the person had the capacity to object to this removal in full knowledge of the potential implications.

8.31. The Law Commission recommended that only minor amendments would be needed to the terminology of place of safety orders to comply with the extended jurisdiction. They were concerned to remove the reference to police stations as an unnecessary source of "protective accommodation".

8.32. The Law Commission recommended that a temporary protection order should be time limited to eight days and should not be capable of extension. Emergency protection orders under the Children Act 1989 may be extended once for a maximum period of seven days.

8.33. The Government accepts the principle of this recommendation but seeks views on whether such orders should be capable of extension and on the need to retain police stations as a form of protective accommodation.

Q97. Should it be possible to extend temporary protection orders?

Q98. Is there a need to retain police stations as a form of protective accommodation?

8.34. The Law Commission recommended that the court could, in the making of such an order, also give directions for assessment where it is necessary. This accords with current practice in the Children Act 1989 and may be necessary to determine what long term plans are appropriate to protect the best interests of the person concerned. The Government therefore accepts this recommendation in principle.

8.35. It was recommended that explicit reference should be made to the need to return the person to the place from which they were removed as soon as it is practicable and consistent with his or her interests. This is consistent with the principles of community care and should go some way to ensuring there is no delay in dealing with the person's ongoing needs. This return must, however, be consistent with the patient's interests – this will cover the situation where the person does not wish to return home or does not feel able to decide.

8.36. The Law Commission recommended that, given the emergency nature of such orders, they must be capable of being made ex parte.

8.37. The views of respondents on this would be welcomed.

Discharge of a temporary protection order

8.38. The Law Commission suggested that the person concerned, any donee of a CPA, and any court appointed manager should be able to apply for the discharge of a temporary protection order where this has been made ex parte. The Law Commission had originally suggested that the person with whom the vulnerable person had been living should also be able to apply – respondents to consultation suggested this was inappropriate because this person may have been the abuser.

8.39. The Government is concerned that these categories of person are too narrow and that to exclude the person with whom the vulnerable person resided may be inappropriate, as they may not have been involved in any abuse. A further question is whether there should be any time limit as to how soon an application for discharge can be made. Under the Children Act 1989, no application for the discharge of an emergency protection order can be made within 72 hours of the order.

> **Q99.** *Should the categories of person able to apply to discharge a temporary protection order be widened?*

> **Q100.** *Should there be a time limit specifying when an application for discharge can be made?*

Appeals

8.40. The Law Commission recommended that, as with emergency protection orders under the Children Act 1989, there should be no need for appeals against these orders, because:

> the person concerned or any substitute decision maker could be heard at the hearing or apply for the discharge of an order where this had been made ex parte; and

> social services authorities could simply apply for a new order with new evidence if they were turned down.

8.41. The views of respondents on this would be welcomed.

An offence of obstruction

8.42. All those who responded in writing to this point, supported the creation of such an offence, as long as it is clear that the vulnerable person him or herself cannot be charged with such an offence. The Law Commission recommended that such an offence should include the obstruction without reasonable cause of an authorised officer in the exercise of his or her powers or any person acting pursuant to a temporary protection or assessment order. It was recommended that such an offence should be summary only, punishable by fine or imprisonment for a maximum of three months. The local authority would have the power to prosecute.

8.43. The views of respondents on this would be welcomed.

MISCELLANEOUS
Power to assist in legal proceedings

8.44. The Law Commission recommended that the local authority should be able to assist the vulnerable person in bringing proceedings under the private law. The Government is not convinced that this is an appropriate function for local authorities and believe that there are other options, such as reference to be made to the court for the appointment of a manager.

> **Q101.** *Should the local authority be able to assist a vulnerable person in bringing proceedings under private law?*

The protection of property

8.45. Under section 47 of the National Assistance Act 1948, the local authority have an obligation to protect the moveable property of people admitted to hospital, or other accommodation. The Law Commission recommended that this obligation should also extend to occasions where a vulnerable person was removed from their home, including temporary protection and assessment orders.

8.46. The Law Commission also recommended that local authorities should have the power to take reasonable steps for the protection of the property and affairs of a person who is without capacity to protect them and for whom the local authority provides alternative accommodation. They stopped short of making this a more extensive duty, as there might be more appropriate ways of doing this, such as a court appointed manager.

8.47. The Government accepts this recommendation in principle, but seeks views on the practicalities of these proposals.

Q102. Are the proposals for the protection of property likely to prove practical?

Guardianship under the Mental Health Act

8.48. The Law Commission provisionally proposed that (subject to minor amendments) the system of guardianship should remain in place to enable those who might otherwise have had to remain in hospital to be able to live in the community. The majority of respondents to consultation agreed with this view.

8.49. The Law Commission did, however, suggest some minor amendments, but did not include them in their draft Bill, given the Department of Health's then recent deliberations on this issue. First, there was a suggestion that the appointment of those currently known as guardians should be restricted to social services authorities and health authorities, given that private individuals' responsibilities would be covered by the wider jurisdiction proposed by the Law Commission. The Law Commission also recommended that a guardian should be given an additional power to convey the patient to a residence specified by the guardian. This was unanimously supported on consultation. The Law Commission also recommended that the powers of the Mental Health Act Commission should be extended to include those received into guardianship. The Department of Health will look at recommendations for changes in guardianship alongside the wider consideration of changes in the Mental Health Act when there is a fundamental review of the Act.

The Judicial Forum

BACKGROUND

9.1. Although jurisdictional questions were ancillary to its substantive proposals for reform of the law, the Law Commission received views on the structure of the judicial forum as part of its consultation process and made certain recommendations in the Report.

9.2. The Government accepts the majority of these recommendations in principle, but seeks views on their practicality in a number of areas.

COURTS OR TRIBUNALS?

9.3. The Law Commission identified three possible options as to the type of judicial forum which would operate the jurisdiction:

a jurisdiction integrating the Court of Protection and exercised by ordinary courts;

a jurisdiction exercised by administrative tribunals;

a hybrid system with medical issues decided by tribunals and the courts deciding all other issues.

9.4. Although favouring the informality which could be offered by tribunals, the Law Commission recommended that the new jurisdiction be operated by the courts, particularly as an informal and inquisitorial approach is adopted by the Court of Protection in any event. Using the courts would have the advantages of:

using existing resources and expertise; and

having an integrated forum for decision making.

9.5. These conclusions were supported in broad terms by the House of Lords Select Committee, who accepted that it would not be practical or desirable to establish a tribunal forum for dealing with health care matters, alongside a court-based forum for considering other matters. Such a proposal would lead to complication and confusion.

9.6. The Government accepts this recommendation in principle, but notes the Select Committee's observation that "some mechanism should be adopted whereby the new court will make full use of appropriate ethical and medical advice"[1]. Views are welcomed on how best this could be achieved.

> **Q103. How could any new forum ensure the best use of appropriate ethical and medical advice?**

Magistrates' courts

9.7. The Law Commission recognised that family proceedings courts currently exercise a specialist jurisdiction in relation to children and other family cases. They suggested that, since specially trained magistrates have built up experience in exercising emergency protective powers under the Children Act 1989, this expertise should be utilised. The Law Commission suggested that the jurisdiction of magistrates' courts should be extended in relation to applications under Part II of their draft Bill (i.e. the granting of warrants and short-term orders in respect of those at risk). In addition, the Law Commission recommended that proceedings under Part II of their draft Bill should be treated as family proceedings.

9.8. The Government accepts this recommendation in principle, and agrees that magistrates should not be required to deal with private law issues arising in this field. This would result in a dilution of the expertise of the judiciary required to deal with these cases.

Constitution

9.9. The Law Commission advocated the establishment of a new superior court of record called the Court of Protection in place of the current Court of Protection. They recommended that the Lord Chancellor should designate a Senior Judge of the Court of Protection and, if in the future the volume of work justified it, a President of the Court of Protection.

9.10. The Government accepts this recommendation in principle, and observes that there would be benefits in maintaining the same name. Some concerns have been expressed, however, as to whether it would be confusing for the new court to retain the name of the current court.

> **Q104. What should any new forum be called?**

Location of the Court of Protection

9.11. The Law Commission noted that many respondents to their Consultation Papers had criticised the Court of Protection's lack of a regional presence. The Law Commission suggested in their report that the new Court of Protection should be based in London but be able to sit in different parts of England and Wales. They suggested that at least one venue be designated for each of the six court circuits in England and Wales.

9.12. In making these recommendations the Law Commission did, however, note that it was hard to quantify the effect of the lack of regional presence of the current Court of Protection. The need for a regional presence would also need to be balanced with the potential impact on currently centralised expertise and resources.

---

1 *HL Paper 21-I, para. 248.*

9.13. It is far from easy to predict the likely caseload that would emerge from these proposals. The Government notes that the Law Commission recommended only that the Court of Protection should have a regional presence, and not the PTO. This would cause difficulties for the PTO, in their role in support of the Court. Creating a regional presence for the PTO would have significant resource implications. The Government is also keen to ensure that the expertise that currently exists in the Court of Protection and the PTO is not diluted. Other factors which would need to be considered are that the development of information technology means that urgent matters can more easily be dealt with promptly at a distance, and over 50% of the patients of the Court of Protection currently live in the South of England.

9.14. The Government therefore intends to adopt the approach taken with other specialist areas of the court system, where resources are centralised until the workload in a particular area justifies a new centre. This is the way mercantile and commercial work is managed in the county court. The Government therefore accepts the Law Commission's recommendation that the Lord Chancellor should take the power to be able to designate additional registries outside London. Views are welcomed on how a regional structure for the Court of Protection would work in practice.

Q105. Are the Government's proposals acceptable?

Judiciary

9.15. The Law Commission recommended that the Lord Chancellor should have the power to provide by order for which kind of judge of the Court of Protection should deal with any particular proceedings and for the transfer of proceedings between the different kinds of judges.

9.16. The Law Commission also suggested that the jurisdiction of the Court of Protection should be exercised by judges nominated by the Lord Chancellor, whether Chancery Division or Family Division High Court Judges, Circuit Judges or District Judges. The need for a range of levels of judiciary to deal with different proceedings at different stages of a case's progress is accepted. It should be noted that the jurisdiction currently operated is very small with only five judicial officers.

9.17. The Government accepts these recommendations. A key factor for the Lord Chancellor in considering the nomination of additional judges will be the need to maintain the high degree of specialisation and expertise that currently exists in this field.

The proceedings

9.18. It is intended that the new statutory decision-making jurisdiction should be available in respect of persons without capacity who have attained the age of sixteen. It is recommended by the Law Commission that, as regards persons who have not attained the age of eighteen, the Lord Chancellor should have the power to provide for the transfer of proceedings between a court having jurisdiction under their proposals and a court having jurisdiction under the Children Act 1989. In respect of sixteen and seventeen year olds, this would allow applicants to choose the most appropriate jurisdiction. The court would also have the power to decline to exercise its jurisdiction if it considered that the case could be dealt with more suitably under the other jurisdiction. The Lord Chancellor would have the power to make orders to effect this. The present jurisdiction over the financial affairs of minors who will remain under a mental incapacity on attaining the age of 18 would remain intact.

9.19. The Government accepts this recommendation in principle.

Applicants

9.20. In its Consultation Papers, the Law Commission suggested that some applicants for private law orders should be able to apply as of right, while others would require leave. The Law Commission noted the difficulty in setting parameters as to who should have an automatic power to make applications. They decided, therefore, to restrict those categories of applicants who should have an automatic right to apply to those who have existing decision-making powers, or are mentioned in an existing order. In addition, the Law Commission advocated the giving of an automatic right to apply to the Public Trustee where he or she has any function that can be exercised by virtue of an existing order.

9.21. The Government is minded to reject this recommendation as:

there is no indication that the current system (where there is no leave to apply) is being abused;

applications for leave may increase delay and cost to vulnerable people, carers and their families and the taxpayer; and

application for leave increases the sense of formality.

9.22. The Law Commission proposed that the new Court of Protection should have the power to make an order or directions on a matter, pending a decision on whether the person concerned is without capacity in relation to that matter. It also recommended that proceedings under the new jurisdiction should be conducted in accordance with rules made by the Lord Chancellor

> **Q106. Should there be a restriction on the categories of applicants with an automatic right to apply?**

Appeals

9.23. The Law Commission recommended that the usual civil appeals system should apply to the new jurisdiction.

9.24. The Government accepts this recommendation in principle.

INDEPENDENT REPORTS

9.25. The Law Commission stated in their report that decisions taken by the court on behalf of a person without capacity should in general be taken in that person's "best interests", including consideration of their wishes and feelings. In circumstances where the person concerned is neither present nor represented, the Law Commission advocated that an independent report be prepared. The Official Solicitor currently prepares reports on adult medical treatment, contact and residence issues in cases under the declaratory jurisdiction of the High Court. As to providing a mechanism by which such a report could be prepared, the Law Commission suggested giving the court the power to ask a probation officer to report to the court or arrange for another person to report on the matters with which the court is concerned. Finally, the Law Commission recommended that the role of the Lord Chancellor's Visitors should be preserved.

9.26. The Government accepts that a reporting function may be desirable, but seeks views on by whom and how this might be conducted. The Government do not regard this as an appropriate function for the Family Court Welfare Service (FCWS). The FCWS is already operating at full capacity, and has no expertise at dealing with mentally incapable adults: their work is restricted exclusively to children. The Lord Chancellor's Visitors have expertise in this area, but there would be considerable resource implications in extending their remit.

Q107. By whom, and how, should reports be prepared?

PRIVACY OF PROCEEDINGS

9.27. At present PVS cases are heard in open court. The court will normally take steps to preserve the anonymity of the patient and the patient's family by making appropriate orders under section 11 of the Contempt of Court Act 1981. The present Rules of the Court of Protection make provision for proceedings to be held in private and for enabling the court to determine who should be admitted, when it sits in private, and excluded, when it sits in public. The Law Commission suggested that this should also be the case for the new jurisdiction.

9.28. In addition, the Law Commission suggested that, as under the Children Act 1989, it should be an offence to publish identifying information about a person involved in incapacity proceedings and that the provisions of the existing law, which render publicity a contempt of court in certain circumstances, should also apply, as they do at present, to proceedings under part VII of the Mental Health Act 1983.

9.29. Two recent cases have helped clarify the law in this area, and support the line suggested by the Law Commission. In *Re G*[2], which concerned a patient in PVS, the President of the Family Division held that there was a legitimate public interest in the issues raised in applications for declarations that the withdrawal of treatment may be lawful. The public interest was such that the hearing of those applications should be in open court. The President confirmed that the parties should be protected from intrusive publicity by means of section 11 of the Contempt of Court Act 1981.

9.30. In the case of *Re C*[3], which also concerned a PVS patient, an order was made prohibiting publication of any details identifying the patient, his parents, other witnesses and the hospital. The Official Solicitor applied to the court for guidance as to whether the order continued in effect following the death of the patient. The President of the Family Division decided that the order must continue after death on the basis that those involved in the case must feel free to do and assert what they regard as in the patient's best interests, without fear of the cloak of anonymity being lifted as soon as the patient dies. The President emphasised that the public

2   Re G (Adult Patient: Publicity) [1996] 1 FCR 413.

3   Re C (Adult Patient: restriction of publicity after death) [1996] Fam Law 610

interest in hearing more about a particular case could always be tested by an express application to the court seeking discharge of the order.

9.31. The Government accepts the principle of the Law Commission's proposals relating to the privacy of proceedings.

Summary of Consultation Questions

CHAPTER ONE: INTRODUCTION

Q1a. What resource implications do those working in this area envisage would result for them and for other parties from the proposals?

Q1b. Would the likely benefits render the costs incurred worthwhile?

Q1c. How should these costs be met?

Q2. Should a common GB-wide approach be given to the health matters covered by the Law Commission and Scottish Law Commission?

Q3. Should the provisions recommended by the Law Commission apply only to those aged 16 or over?

CHAPTER TWO: BACKGROUND

Q4. Do respondents have any concerns regarding the Law Commission's recommendations in so far as the ECHR is concerned?

CHAPTER THREE: THE KEY PRINCIPLES: CAPACITY, BEST INTERESTS, AND THE GENERAL AUTHORITY TO ACT REASONABLY

Q5a. Is the proposed definition of incapacity appropriate, and likely to be of use to practitioners?

Q5b. If so, how do practitioners see this working in practice?

Q6. How, in practice, should "all practicable steps" be defined?

Q7. When would it be reasonable to conclude that such steps had been taken?

Q8. How best can consistency be ensured in the determining of inability to make a decision?

Q9. Do the Law Commission's definitions of inability to make a decision offer sufficient guidance for medical practitioners?

Q10. Is the best interests approach the most appropriate for making decisions on behalf of mentally incapacitated adults?

Q11. Is the proposed guidance for deciding what is in a person's best interests appropriate?

In particular:

    i.   how should the decision-maker deal with differences of opinion between those who are to be consulted?

    ii. will the medical profession be subject to accusations of negligence if they fail to make proper enquiries to identify or locate all interested parties?

    iii. can we always expect relatives and carers to put the interests of the person without capacity entirely before their own, especially if their own welfare or that of another relative or close friend is at stake?

    iv. should the guidance take into account religious or cultural factors in establishing a person's best interests? If so, how could this most effectively be done?

Q12. Is the Law Commission definition of the general authority satisfactory? If not, how should it be amended?

Q13a. Are additional safeguards required to ensure the "necessaries" rule does not lead to abuses?

Q13b. If so, what additional safeguards might be incorporated?

Q14. How would a release of payments scheme work in practice? In particular

    i   will sufficient institutions and individuals be willing to participate in the scheme to make it workable?

    ii. will there need to be an obligation on companies to check that the information provided is valid?

    iii. will doctors fully understand the financial implications of the medical certificate they are preparing?

    iv. will there be a need for appropriate witnessing or authorising of the medical certificate to prevent fraud?

    v. is the proposed limit of £2000 per year realistic and practical? If not, what should be the limit?

Q15. Should direct payments to third parties be restricted to "necessaries" only?

Q16. What are the respective merits of the Law Commission's scheme at paragraphs 3.32 – 3.37 and the Scottish proposals at paragraph 3.39? In particular:

   i.   is it desirable to have a common scheme for Scotland and England and Wales?

   ii.   is it desirable to have the additional protection for the funds of the person without capacity that is provided by the public guardian in the Scottish proposals, recognising that the public guardian role will require to be funded?

   iii. who would perform the role of the public guardian, should the Scottish proposals be adopted for England and Wales?

Q17. Should the interests of a child continue to take precedence over those of the person without capacity in relation to a child's property?

Q18. What type of guidance might be helpful for carers?

CHAPTER FOUR: ADVANCE STATEMENTS ABOUT HEALTH CARE

Q19. Should the Government legislate in the area of advance statements?

Q20. What should be the objective of legislation on advance statements?

Q21. Would the safeguards be sufficient to ensure that advance statements did not unintentionally prevent the use of medical procedures developed since the drafting of the statement?

Q22. Is this an appropriate definition of an advance refusal?

Q23. How best could safeguards be put in place to ensure advance statements are the result of a choice that is informed, considered, and free from undue influence?

Q24. Should advance refusals apply to all cases?

Q25. If in general advance statements overrule the decision-making of someone granted general authority, in what circumstances (if any) should there be an exception to this rule?

Q26. Should an advance refusal only apply when the life of the patient is in danger if the refusal has specifically acknowledged the risk of death?

Q27a. Should a woman need to refer specifically to pregnancy in order for an advance refusal to apply during pregnancy?

Q27b. Should advance refusals concerning treatment in childbirth only apply when the life of the patient is in danger if the refusal has specifically acknowledged the risk of death?

Q28. Would these recommendations provide an appropriate balance between protecting health care providers, and protecting patients?

Q29. In what form or forms should an advance statement be recorded in order to be valid?

Q30. Should an advance refusal be able to refuse "basic care"?

Q31. How should "basic care" be defined?

Q32. Should a person who has made an appropriate advance refusal be administered direct oral nutrition and hydration against their objections (force fed)?

Q33. Would the courts be the most appropriate forum for deciding on the validity or applicability of an advance statement?

Q34. Should there be a specific offence of concealing or destroying a written advance refusal of treatment with intent to deceive?

CHAPTER FIVE: INDEPENDENT SUPERVISION OF MEDICAL AND RESEARCH PROCEDURES

Q35. Should an attorney be able to consent to medical procedures which would otherwise require the approval of the court?

Q36. Should an attorney ever be able to refuse treatment?

Q37a. Should the court be asked to rule on all proposed sterilisations for contraceptive purposes?

Q37b. Should the court be asked to rule on all proposed sterilisations to relieve the existing detrimental effects of menstruation?

Q37c. Should the court be asked to rule on all treatment for diseases where the treatment will, or is reasonably likely to, render the person permanently infertile?

Q38. Should the donation of any organs be excluded from this general rule?

Q39a. Should it ever be necessary to consider an incapacitated person as a donor of regenerative tissue?

Q39b. If so, should there be procedural safeguards similar to those which exist for non-regenerative tissue or bone marrow?

Q40. Do the proposals for a second medical opinion provide a sufficient safeguard in relation to:

  i.   sterilisation to relieve the existing detrimental effects of menstruation;

  ii.   abortion; or

  iii. treatment for medical disorder?

Q41. The Government would welcome views on other procedures which should be added to the list proposed by the Law Commission.

Q42. Should the discontinuation of artificial nutrition and hydration be lawful for defined patients if certain statutory criteria are met?

Q43. Is "patients who have no prospect of recovery who are either unconscious or in a permanent vegetative state" a suitable definition?

Q44a. Should the court retain the exclusive right to make decisions on the withdrawal of artificial nutrition or hydration, or

Q44b. should a person acting under a power of attorney be able to make such decisions? or

Q44c. could these decisions appropriately be made by the second opinion procedure?

Q45. If either of the alternatives to the court retaining exclusive rights is considered appropriate, are any additional safeguards necessary in order to protect the patient?

Q46. In considering the continuance or withdrawal from PVS patients of artificial nutrition and hydration, should regard be given to the best interests guidance?

Q47. Are there any circumstances in which it is ethical and reasonable to apply to patients unable to give consent medical procedures of benefit to others?

Q48. Should research procedures not intended to benefit the patient be allowed?

Q49. Are the safeguards proposed by the Council of Europe adequate to ensure that any scheme would not be open to abuse?

Q50. What, if any, additional safeguards would be required?

Q51. What benefits would a Mental Incapacity Research Committee provide over and above those provided by Local and Multi-Centre Research Ethics Committees?

CHAPTER SIX: CONTINUING POWERS OF ATTORNEY
Q52. Should the Government legislate to create a power of attorney so that the attorney is able to make decisions on health-care matters?

Q53. What safeguards would be needed to ensure these recommendations would work in practice?

Q54. Would safeguards be needed to ensure that such a recommendation would work in practice?

Q55. Should a person between the ages of 16 and 18 be permitted to be a donor?

Q56. Would such a recommendation be workable in practice?

Q57. What provision should be made for people who have reading difficulties or whose first language is not English?

Q58. Should a CPA be able to grant general authority, or should specific matters be listed on the form?[1]

Q59. Should there be a system for certification of CPAs by a solicitor and/or a medical practitioner?

Q60. What safeguards should accompany a registration system for CPAs?

Q61. Would the Public Trust Office be the most appropriate registering authority?

Q62. What structure and function should the registering authority take?

Q63. What safeguards should be implemented to minimise the risk of fraudulent registration?

Q64. What period of notice should be allowed between notification of registration and the ability to use the power of attorney?

Q65. What proof of service of notification should be required before an attorney is authorised to act?

Q66. Should the functions of the registering authority be administrative only?

Q67. Under what circumstances should the court *not* be able to cure defects in a CPA?

Q68. Is there a need for an option to convert an EPA into a CPA?

CHAPTER SEVEN: DECISION-MAKING BY THE COURT

Q69. Should there be a single court jurisdiction, able to deal with all areas of decision-making (financial, welfare, and health care)?

Q70. Does the current Court of Protection offer the most appropriate base for such a jurisdiction?

Q71. Should legislation in this area include a "no order" principle?

Q72a. Should any decision-making forum have the power to declare:

    i.   whether or not a person has capacity; or

    ii. whether or not an advance statement is valid; or

    iii. whether or not authority (such as a CPA) should be delegated?

---

1 *As recommended by the Law Commission in para. 7.13 of Consultation Paper 128.*

Q72b. If so, how should such a declaration cater for the needs of those with fluctuating conditions, such as manic depression, where the person concerned may have unpredictable periods of complete lucidity when substitute decision-making is not required?

Q73. Should the court be able to appoint a manager?

Q74. If so, what should be the scope of a manager's responsibilities?

Q75. What criteria should be used to decide who should be a manager?

Q76. Are there any circumstances in which the discretion of the court in these areas should be limited?

Q77. Should explicit provision be made for other orders in addition to residence and contact orders?

Q78. Should a court-appointed manager have the power to refuse consent to particular forms of health care?

Q79. Should a manager be able to consent to non-therapeutic research procedures?

Q80. Is there a need for a new provision for compulsory admission to hospital?

Q81. Is there a need for time limited appointments in the majority of cases, or might the disadvantages of this in terms of expense and possible inconvenience outweigh any likely advantages?

Q82. Would these recommendations work in practice?

Q83. Are these recommendations workable in practice?

Q84. Would the recommendations relating to the supervisory role of the Public Trustee work in practice?

Q85. How would the recommendation that managers be remunerated operate where the incapacitated adult has no finances? In particular, what funding mechanism should be put in place?

Q86. Is there a need for a Code of Practice in this area, and, if so, what should be included in such a code?

Q87a. Should there be a general assumption that care home managers should not be appointed as managers of an incapable adult's financial affairs?

Q87b. Are there circumstances in which, despite the conflict of interest, a care home manager might be the most suitable person?

Q88. If care home managers are to be allowed to carry out this role, what approval and monitoring systems should there be?

CHAPTER EIGHT: PUBLIC LAW PROTECTION FOR PEOPLE AT RISK

Q89. Is there a need for legislation in this area?

Q90. Is the proposed definition of harm appropriate?

Q91. Should social services authorities be required to investigate allegations of abuse or neglect of an incapacitated, mentally disordered or vulnerable adult?

Q92. Should any other organisations, such as the police, hospital managers, or the trustees of charities, be given a similar power?

Q93. Is it appropriate or practical for social services authorities (or any other organisation that it is thought should conduct investigations) to nominate authorised officers?

Q94a. Should there be provision for telescoping these procedures in certain circumstances?

Q94b. How might such telescoping work?

Q95. Are there any circumstances in which the period of eight days should be extended?

Q96. How would removal from the home work in practice?

Q97. Should it be possible to extend temporary protection orders?

Q98. Is there a need to retain police stations as a form of protective accommodation?

Q99. Should the categories of person able to apply to discharge a temporary protection order be widened?

Q100. Should there be a time limit specifying when an application for discharge can be made?

Q101. Should the local authority be able to assist a vulnerable person in bringing proceedings under private law?

Q102. Are the proposals for the protection of property likely to prove practical?

CHAPTER NINE: JUDICIAL FORUM

Q103. How could any new forum ensure the best use of appropriate ethical and medical advice?

Q104. What should any new forum be called?

Q105. Are the Government's proposals acceptable?

Q106. Should there be a restriction on the categories of applicant with an automatic right to apply?

Q107. By whom, and how, should reports be prepared?

annex

The Law Commission's Recommendations

PART II – THE CONTEXT AND THE BASIC APPROACH TO REFORM

1. We recommend the introduction of a single piece of legislation to make new provision for people who lack mental capacity: and to confer new functions on local authorities in relation to people in need of care or protection. (Paragraph 2.51 and draft Mental Incapacity Bill.)

2. The provisions of the legislation should in general apply to those aged 16 and over. (Paragraph 2.52 and Draft Bill, clauses 1(2) and 36(2).)

3. The Secretary of State should prepare and from time to time revise a code or codes of practice to give guidance in connection with the legislation. There should be consultation before any code is prepared or revised, and preparation of any part of any code may be delegated. (Paragraph 2.53 and draft Bill, clause 31(1) and (2).)

PART III – TWO FUNDAMENTAL CONCEPTS: LACK OF CAPACITY AND BEST INTERESTS

4. There should be a presumption against lack of capacity and any question whether a person lacks capacity should be decided on the balance of probabilities. (Paragraph 3.2 and draft Bill, clause 2(6).)

5. The expression "mental disability" in the new legislation should mean any disability or disorder of the mind or brain, whether permanent or temporary, which results in an impairment or disturbance of mental functioning. (Paragraphs 3.8 to 3.12 and draft Bill, clause 2(2).)

6. Legislation should provide that a person is without capacity if at the material time he or she is:

1) unable by reason of mental disability to make a decision on the matter in question, or

2) unable to communicate a decision on that matter because he or she is unconscious or for any other reason. (Paragraph 3.14 and draft Bill, clause 2(1).)

7. A person should be regarded as unable to make a decision by reason of mental disability if the disability is such that, at the time when the decision needs to be made, he or she is unable to understand or retain the information relevant to the decision, including information about the reasonably foreseeable consequences of deciding one way or another or failing to make the decision. (Paragraph 3.16 and draft Bill, clause 2(2)(a).)

8. A person should be regarded as unable to make a decision by reason of mental disability if the disability is such that, at the time when the decision needs to be made, he or she is unable to make a decision based on the information relevant to the decision, including information about the reasonably foreseeable consequences of deciding one way or another or failing to make the decision. (Paragraph 3.17 and draft Bill, clause 2(2)(b).)

9. A person should not be regarded as unable to understand the information relevant to a decision if he or she is able to understand an explanation of that information in broad terms and simple language. (Paragraph 3.18 and draft Bill, clause 2(3).)

10. A person should not be regarded as unable to make a decision by reason of mental disability merely because he or she makes a decision which would not be made by a person of ordinary prudence. (Paragraph 3.19 and draft Bill, clause 2(4).)

11. A person should not be regarded as unable to communicate his or her decision unless all practicable steps to enable him or her to do so have been taken without success. (Paragraph 3.21 and draft Bill, clause 2(5).)

12. The Secretary of State should prepare and from time to time revise a code of practice for the guidance of persons assessing whether a person is or is not without capacity to make a decision or decisions on any matter. (Paragraph 3.22 and draft Bill, clause 31(1)(a).)

13. Anything done for, and any decision made on behalf of, a person without capacity should be done or made in the best interests of that person. (Paragraph 3.25 and draft Bill, clause 3(1).)

14. In deciding what is in a person's best interests regard should be had to:-

1) the ascertainable past and present wishes and feelings of the person concerned, and the factors that person would consider if able to do so;

2) the need to permit and encourage the person to participate, or to improve his or her ability to participate, as fully as possible in anything done for and any decision affecting him or her;

3) the views of other people whom it is appropriate and practicable to consult about the person's wishes and feelings and what would be in his or her best interests;

4) whether the purpose for which any action or decision is required can be as effectively achieved in a manner less restrictive of the person's freedom of action. (Paragraphs 3.26 to 3.37 and draft Bill, clause 3(2).)

PART IV – GENERAL AUTHORITY TO ACT REASONABLY

15. It should be lawful to do anything for the personal welfare or health care of a person who is, or is reasonably believed to be, without capacity in relation to the matter in question if it is in all the circumstances reasonable for it to be done by the person who does it. (Paragraphs 4.1 to 4.4 and draft Bill, clause 4(1).)

16. Where necessary goods are supplied to, or necessary services are provided for, a person without capacity to contract, he or she must pay a reasonable price for them. (Paragraph 4.9 and draft Bill, clause 34(1).)

17. Where reasonable actions for the personal welfare or health care of the person lacking capacity involve expenditure, it shall be lawful for the person who is taking the action (1) to pledge the other's credit for that purpose or (2) to apply money in the possession of the person concerned for meeting the expenditure; and if the person taking the action bears the expenditure then he or she is entitled to be reimbursed or otherwise indemnified from the money of the person concerned. (Paragraph 4.10 and draft Bill, clause 4(2).)

18. There should be a statutory scheme enabling certain payments which would otherwise be made to a person without capacity to be made instead to a person acting on his or her behalf. (Paragraphs 4.12 to 4.21 and draft Bill, clause 4(4) and Schedule 1.)

19. No person should be able to make decisions about the following matters on behalf of a person without capacity:

1) consent to marriage,

2) consent to have sexual relations,

3) consent to a divorce petition on the basis of two years separation,

4) agreement to adoption or consent to freeing a child for adoption,

5) voting at an election for any public office or

6) discharging parental responsibilities except in relation to a child's property. (Paragraph 4.29 and draft Bill, clause 30.)

20. The general authority to provide care to a person without capacity should not authorise the use or threat of force to enforce the doing of anything to which that person objects; nor should it authorise the detention or confinement of that person, whether or not he or she objects. This provision is not to preclude the taking of steps which are necessary to avert a substantial risk of serious harm to the person concerned. (Paragraphs 4.30 to 4.33 and draft Bill, clause 5.)

21. The general authority should not authorise the doing of anything which is contrary to the directions of, or inconsistent with a decision made by, an attorney or manager acting within the scope of his or her authority. However, this restriction will not apply to actions necessary to prevent the death of, or a serious deterioration in the condition of, the person concerned while an order is being sought from the court. (Paragraph 4.34 and draft Bill, clause 6.)

22. The Secretary of State should prepare and from time to time revise a code of practice for the guidance of persons acting in pursuance of the general authority o act and the statutory restrictions which apply to it. (Paragraph 4.37 and draft Bill, clause 31(1)(b).)

23. It should be an offence for anyone to ill-treat or wilfully neglect a person in relation to whom he or she has powers by virtue of the new legislation. (Paragraph 4.38 and draft Bill, clause 32(1).)

PART V – ADVANCE STATEMENTS ABOUT HEALTH CARE

24. An "advance refusal of treatment" should be defined as a refusal made by a person aged eighteen or over with the necessary capacity of any medical, surgical or dental treatment or other procedure and intended to have effect at any subsequent time when he or she may be without capacity to give or refuse consent. (Paragraph 5.16 and draft Bill, clause 9(1).)

25. The general authority should not authorise any treatment or procedure if an advance refusal of treatment by the person concerned applies to that treatment or procedure in the circumstances of the case. (Paragraph 5.20 and draft Bill, clause 9(2).)

26. In the absence of any indication to the contrary it shall be presumed that an advance refusal of treatment does not apply in circumstances where those having the care of the person who made it consider that the refusal (a) endangers that person's life or (b) if that person is a woman who is pregnant, the life of the foetus. (Paragraphs 5.23 to 5.26 and draft Bill, clause 9(3).)

27. No person should incur liability (1) for the consequences of withholding any treatment or procedure if he or she has reasonable grounds for believing that an advance refusal of treatment applies; or (2) for carrying out any treatment or procedure to which an advance refusal applies unless he or she knows or has reasonable grounds for believing that an advance refusal applies. (Paragraph 5.27 and draft Bill, clause 9(4).)

28. In the absence of any indication to the contrary it should be presumed that an advance refusal was validly made if it is in writing, signed and witnessed. (Paragraphs 5.29 to 5.30 and draft Bill, clause 9(5).)

29. An advance refusal of treatment may at any time be withdrawn or altered by the person who made it, if he or she has capacity to do so. (Paragraphs 5.31 to 5.32 and draft Bill, clause 9(6).)

30. An advance refusal of treatment should not preclude the provision of "basic care", namely care to maintain bodily cleanliness and to alleviate severe pain, as well as the provision of direct oral nutrition and hydration. (Paragraph 5.34 and draft Bill, clause 9(7)(a) and (8).)

31. An advance refusal should not preclude the taking of any action necessary to prevent the death of the maker or a serious deterioration in his or her condition pending a decision of the court on the validity or applicability of an advance refusal or on the question whether it has been withdrawn or altered. (Paragraph 5.36 and draft Bill, clause 9(7)(b).)

32. It should be an offence punishable with a maximum of two years imprisonment to conceal or

destroy a written advance refusal of treatment with intent to deceive. (Paragraphs 5.38 and draft Bill, clause 33.)

PART VI – INDEPENDENT SUPERVISION OF MEDICAL AND RESEARCH PROCEDURES

33. The general authority should not authorise certain listed treatments or procedures, which will require authorisation by the court or the consent of an attorney or manager. (Paragraph 6.3 and draft Bill, clause 7(1).)

34. Any treatment or procedure intended or reasonably likely to render the person permanently infertile should require court authorisation unless it is to treat a disease of the reproductive organs or relieve existing detrimental effects of menstruation. (Paragraph 6.4 and draft Bill, clause 7(2)(a).)

35. Any treatment or procedure to facilitate the donation of non-regenerative tissue or bone marrow should require court authorisation. (Paragraph 6.5 and draft Bill, clause 7(2)(b).)

36. The Secretary of State should have power to prescribe further treatments requiring court authorisation. (Paragraph 6.6 and draft Bill, clause 7(2)(c).)

37. The general authority should not authorise certain listed treatments or procedures, which should require a certificate from an independent doctor appointed for that purpose by the Secretary of State or the consent of an attorney or manager. The independent doctor should certify that the person concerned is without capacity to consent but that it is in his or her best interests for the treatment or procedure to be carried out. This should not preclude action necessary to prevent the death of the person concerned or a serious deterioration in his or her condition while the certificate or consent is sought. (Paragraphs 6.7 to 6.8 and draft Bill, clause 8(1), (2) and (6).)

38. Any treatment or procedure intended or reasonably likely to render the person concerned permanently infertile should require a certificate from an independent medical practitioner where it is for relieving the existing detrimental effects of menstruation. (Paragraph 6.9 and draft Bill, clause 8(3)(d).)

39. Abortion should require a certificate from an independent medical practitioner. (Paragraphs 6.10 and draft Bill, clause 8(3)(c).)

40. The treatments for mental disorder described in section 58(1) of the Mental Health Act 1983 should require a certificate from an independent medical practitioner. (Paragraphs 6.11 to 6.14 and draft Bill, clause 8(3)(a) and (b).)

41. The Secretary of State should have power to prescribe that other treatments or procedures should be included in the second opinion category. (Paragraphs 6.15 and draft Bill, clause 8(3((e).)

42. Discontinuing the artificial nutrition and hydration of a patient who is unconscious, has no activity in the cerebral cortex and no prospect of recovery should be lawful if certain statutory requirements are met. (Paragraphs 6.17 to 6.20 and draft Bill, clause 10(1).)

43. The discontinuance of artificial sustenance to an unconscious patient with no activity in the cerebral cortex and no prospect of recovery should require either (1) the approval of the court, (2) the consent of an attorney or manager or (3) if an order of the Secretary of State so provides, a certificate by an independent medical practitioner. (Paragraph 6.21 and draft Bill, clause 10(2).)

44. Where the court, an attorney, a manager or an independent medical practitioner decides on discontinuance of artificial sustenance for an unconscious patient with no activity in the cerebral cortex and no prospect of recovery, then regard must be had to the factors in the best interests checklist. (Paragraph 6.22 and draft Bill, clause 10(3).)

45. The Secretary of State may make an order providing for the carrying out of a procedure in relation to a person without capacity to consent if the procedure, although not carried out for the benefit of that person, will not cause him or her significant harm and will be of significant benefit to others. (Paragraphs 6.23 to 6.26 and draft Bill, clause 10(4).)

46. Research which is unlikely to benefit a participant, or whose benefit is likely to be long delayed, should be lawful in relation to a person without capacity to consent if (1) the research is into an incapacitating condition with which the participant is or may be affected and (2) certain statutory procedures are complied with. (Paragraphs 6.28 to 6.31 and draft Bill, clause 11(1).)

47. There should be a statutory committee to be known as the Mental Incapacity Research Committee. (Paragraph 6.33 and draft Bill, clause 11(2).)

48. The committee may approve proposed research if satisfied:

    1) that it is desirable to provide knowledge of the causes or treatment of, or of the care of people affected by, the incapacitating condition with which any participant is or may be affected,

    2) that the object of the research cannot be effectively achieved without the participation of persons who are or may be without capacity to consent, and

    3) that the research will not expose a participant to more than negligible risk, will not be unduly invasive or restrictive of a participant and will not unduly interfere with a participant's freedom of action or privacy. (Paragraph 6.34 and draft Bill, clause 11(3).)

49. In addition to the approval of the Mental Incapacity Research Committee, non-therapeutic research in relation to a person without capacity should require either:

    1) court approval,

    2) the consent of an attorney or manager,

3)   a certificate from a doctor not involved in the research that the participation of the person is appropriate, or

4)   designation of the research as not involving direct contact. (Paragraphs 6.36 to 6.37 and draft Bill, clause 11(1)(c) and (4).)

PART VII – CONTINUING POWERS OF ATTORNEY

50.   A new form of power of attorney, to be called a "continuing power of attorney" ("CPA"), should be introduced. The donee of a CPA should have authority to make and implement decisions on behalf of the donor which the donor is without capacity to make. (Paragraphs 7.1 to 7.6 and draft Bill, clause 12(1) and (2).)

51.   A CPA may extend to matters relating to a donor's personal welfare, health care and property and affairs (including the conduct of legal proceedings); and may be subject to conditions or restrictions. (Paragraphs 7.7 and draft Bill, clause 16.(1).)

52.   Where an instrument purports to create a CPA but does not comply with the statutory requirements it should confer no powers on the donee. (Paragraph 7.9 and draft Bill, clause 12(4).)

53.   An attorney acting under a Continuing Power of Attorney should act in the best interests of the donor, having regard to the statutory factors. (Paragraph 7.10 and draft Bill, clause 3.)

54.   The restriction against coercion or confinement should apply equally to attorneys. (Paragraph 7.13 and draft Bill, clauses 16(4) and 5.)

55.   No attorney may consent to or refuse any treatment unless the donor is, or is reasonably believed by the attorney to be, without capacity to give or refuse personal consent to that treatment. (Paragraph 7.14 and draft Bill, clause 16(3)(a).)

56.   No attorney should have power to consent to the donor's admission to hospital for assessment or treatment for mental disorder, where such admission is against the will of the donor. (Paragraph 7.15 and draft Bill, clause 16(3)(b).)

57.   No attorney should be authorised to withhold basic care from the donor or refuse consent to its provision. (Paragraph 7.16 and draft Bill, clauses 16(3)(c) and 9(8).)

58.   Unless expressly authorised to do so, no attorney may consent to any treatment refused by the donor by an advance refusal of treatment. (Paragraph 7.17 and draft Bill, clause 16(3)(d)(i).)

59.   Unless expressly authorised to do so, no attorney may consent on a donor's behalf to:

1)   a procedure requiring court approval,

2)   a procedure requiring a certificate from an independent medical practitioner,

3) discontinuance of artificial nutrition or hydration,

4) procedures for the benefit of others, or

5) participation in non-therapeutic research. (Paragraph 7.18 and draft Bill, clause 16(3)(d)(ii) and (5).)

60. Unless expressly authorised to do so, no attorney may refuse consent to any treatment necessary to sustain life. (Paragraph 7.19 and draft Bill, clause 16(3)(d)(iii).)

61. A CPA may only be created by an individual who has attained the age of eighteen. (Paragraph 7.20 and draft Bill, clause 14(1).)

62. An individual donee of a CPA may be described as the holder for the time being of a specified office or position. (Paragraph 7.21 and draft Bill, clause 14(3).)

63. A donor may, in a CPA, appoint a person to replace the donee in the event of the donee disclaiming, dying, becoming bankrupt or becoming divorced from the donor. (Paragraph 7.22 and draft Bill, clause 20(1).)

64. A CPA must contain a statement by the donee that he or she understands the duty to act in the best interests of the donor in relation to any decision which the donor is, or is reasonably believed by the donee to be, without capacity to make. (Paragraph 7.24 and draft Bill, clause 13(3)(b)(ii).)

65. A CPA may be expressed to confer general authority on a donee. (Paragraph 7.25 and draft Bill, clause 16(2).)

66. No document should create a Continuing Power of Attorney until it has been registered in the prescribed manner. (Paragraphs 7.28 to 7.31 and draft Bill, clause 15(1).)

67. A registration authority appointed by the Lord Chancellor should register CPAs. (Paragraphs 7.32 and draft Bill, clause 15(1).)

68. If a donor objects to registration of a CPA then the registration authority should inform the donee and should not register the document unless the court directs it to do so. (Paragraph 7.34 and draft Bill, clause 15(4).)

69. Once a CPA has been registered the registration authority should give notice of that fact in the prescribed form to the donor. (Paragraph 7.36 and draft Bill, clause 15(6)(a).)

70. Once a CPA has been registered the registration authority should give notice of that fact in the prescribed form to a maximum of two people (not including the donee) as specified in the CPA. (Paragraph 7.38 and draft Bill, clause 15(6)(b).)

71. No disclaimer of a registered CPA should be valid unless notice is given to the donor and the registration authority. (Paragraph 7.41 and draft Bill, clause 15(7).)

72.   There should be an express provision that nothing in the legislation should preclude the donor of a CPA from revoking it at any time when he or she has the capacity to do so. (Paragraphs 7.42 to 7.43 and draft Bill, clause 12(3).)

73.   Section 5 of the Powers of Attorney Act 1971 should apply to Continuing Powers of Attorney. (Paragraph 7.44 and draft Bill, clause 19(6).)

74.   Any part of a CPA which relates to matters other than property and financial affairs should not be revoked by the donor's bankruptcy. (Paragraph 7.47 and draft Bill, clause 16(6).)

75.   In the absence of a contrary intention, the appointment of the donee's spouse as an attorney under a CPA should be revoked by the subsequent dissolution or annulment of the parties' marriage. (Paragraph 7.48 and draft Bill, clause 14(5).)

      The registration authority should cancel the registration of a CPA on receipt of a revocation by the donor, a disclaimer by the donee or evidence that the power has expired or been revoked by death, bankruptcy, winding up or the dissolution of the parties' marriage. (Paragraph 7.49 and draft Bill, clause 18(1).)

76.   The registration authority should attach an appropriate note to any registered CPA which has been partially revoked, or in relation to which a replacement donee has gained power to act. (Paragraph 7.49 and draft Bill, clause 18(2) and (5).)

77.   The court should have power to declare that a document not in the prescribed form shall be treated as if it were in that form if the court is satisfied that the persons executing it intended to create a CPA. (Paragraph 7.55 and draft Bill, clause 17(1).)

78.   Subject to any contrary intention expressed in the document, the court should have power to appoint a donee in substitution for in addition to the donee mentioned in a CPA. The court may act where the donor is without capacity to act and the court thinks it desirable to do so. (Paragraph 7.56 and draft Bill, clause 17(3)(c)(i).)

79.   Subject to any contrary intention expressed in the document, the court should have power to modify or extend the scope of the donee's power to act. The court may act where the donor is without capacity to act and the court thinks it desirable to do so. (Paragraph 7.57 and draft Bill, clause 17(3)(c)(ii).)

80.   The court may, on behalf of a donor without capacity to do so, either direct that a purported CPA should not be registered or revoke a CPA where the donee or intended donee has behaved, is behaving or proposes to behave in a way that (1) contravenes or would contravene the authority granted in the CPA or (2) is not or would not be in the donor's best interests. (Paragraph 7.58 and draft Bill, clause 17(6)(b).)

81.   No EPA should be created after the coming into force of the new law in relation to CPAs. Transitional provisions should apply to any EPAs made prior to repeal of the 1985 Act. (Paragraph 7.59 and draft Bill, clause 21(1) and (3); Schedule 3, Parts II to V.)

82. An unregistered EPA may be converted into a CPA by the donor and donee executing a prescribed form and by registration. (Paragraph 7.61 and draft Bill, clause 21(2); Schedule 3, Part I.)

PART VIII – DECISION-MAKING BY THE COURT

83. The court should have power to make a declaration in relation to: (1) the capacity of a person; (2) the validity or applicability of an advance refusal of treatment. (Paragraph 8.8 and draft Bill, clause 23.)

84. The court may

1) make any decision on behalf of a person who lacks capacity to make that decision or

2) appoint a person to be responsible for making a decision on behalf of a person who lacks capacity to make it. (Paragraph 98.9 and draft Bill, clause 24(1).)

The decisions in question may extend to any matter relating to the personal welfare, health care, property or affairs of the person concerned including the conduct of legal proceedings. (Paragraph 8.9 and draft Bill, clause 24(3).)

85. A specific decision by the court is to be preferred to the appointment of a manager. (Paragraph 8.12 and draft Bill, clause 24(2).)

86. The powers conferred on a manager should be as limited in scope and duration as possible. (Paragraph 8.13 and draft Bill, clause 24(2).)

87. The court may make any order or appointment which is in the best interests of the person concerned, regardless of the terms of the application made to the court. (Paragraph 8.14 and draft Bill, clause 24(5).)

88. The court's powers should cover (1) where the person concerned is to live and (2) what contact, if any, the person concerned is to have with specified persons. (Paragraph 8.16 and draft Bill, clause 25(1) (a) and (b).)

89. The court should have power to make an order restraining a person from having contact with or molesting the person without capacity. (Paragraph 8.17 and draft Bill, clause 25(3).)

90. The court's powers should cover the exercise of a person's statutory rights to information. (Paragraph 8.20 and draft Bill, clause 25(1)(c).)

91. The court's powers should cover obtaining statutory benefits and services which may be available to the person concerned. (Paragraph 8.21 and draft Bill, clause 25(1)(d).)

92. The court's powers in relation to health care matters should cover (1) approving or refusing approval for particular forms of health care (2) appointing a manager to consent or refuse consent to particular forms of health care, (3) requiring a person to allow a different person to take over responsibility for the health care of the person concerned. (Paragraph 8.22 and draft Bill, clause 26(1)(a) and (b).)

93. The court's powers should cover obtaining access to the health records of the person concerned. (Paragraph 8.23 and draft Bill, clause 26(1)(c).)

94. The court may not approve, nor a manager consent to, (1) the withholding of basic care, or (2) any treatment refused by an advance refusal of treatment. (Paragraph 8.24 and draft Bill, clause 26(2)(b).)

95. The court may grant a manager express authority to consent to the carrying out of treatments which would otherwise require court approval or a certificate from an independent medical practitioner; or to consent to the carrying out of non-therapeutic procedures or research. (Paragraph 8.26 and draft Bill, clause 26(3).)

96. The court should have power to order the admission to hospital for assessment or treatment for mental disorder of a person without capacity, if satisfied on the evidence of two doctors that:

1) the grounds for admission specified in sections 2 and 3 respectively of the Mental Health Act 1983 exist, and

2) it is appropriate, having regard to the "best interests" factors, that the person concerned should be admitted to hospital. (Paragraphs 8.27 to 8.29 and draft Bill, clause 26(4) and (5).)

97. The court's powers in relation to property and affairs may be exercised where the person concerned is under 16, if it is likely that the person will still lack capacity on attaining his or her majority. (Paragraph 8.32 and draft Bill, clause 27(3).)

98. The court's powers over the property and affairs of a person without capacity should cover;

control and management of any property

the disposal of any property

the carrying on of a business, trade or profession

the dissolution of any partnership

the carrying out of any contract

the discharge of any debt or obligation. (Paragraphs 8.33 and draft Bill, clause 27(1)(a) – (g).)

99. The court's powers should also extend to:

making a settlement of any property, whether with the person concerned or with others as beneficiary or beneficiaries making a will

exercising powers vested in the person concerned.

These powers should not be exercisable by any manager. (Paragraph 8.34 and draft Bill, clause 27(l)(h) – (j) and (2).)

100. A manager may be appointed to take possession on control of all or any specified part of the property of the person concerned and to exercise all or any specified powers in respect of it including such powers of investment as the court may determine. (Paragraph 8.40 and draft Bill, clause 28(7).)

101. An individual appointed as manager may be described as the holder for the time being of an office or position. (Paragraph 8.42 and draft Bill, clause 28(2).)

102. The court may appoint joint, joint and several, successive or standby managers. (Paragraph 8.43 and draft Bill, clause 28(5).)

103. A manager should act in the best interests of the person without capacity, having regard to the statutory factors. (Paragraph 8.44 and draft Bill, clause 3.)

104. A manager should be regarded as the agent of the person for whom he or she is appointed. (Paragraph 8.45 and draft Bill, clause 28(8).)

105. No manager should have power to make a decision which is inconsistent with a decision made within the scope of his or her authority by the donee of a CPA. (Paragraph 8.46 and draft Bill, clause 28(10).)

106. No manager should be appointed for longer than five years. (Paragraph 8.47 and draft Bill, clause 28(4).)

107. The court may require a manager to give to the Public Trustee such security as the court thinks fit, and to submit to the Public Trustee such reports at such intervals as the court thinks fit. (Paragraph 8.48 and draft Bill, clause 28(6)(a).)

108. The Public Trustee should have such supervisory functions in relation to other managers as are laid down in Rules. (Paragraph 8.50 and draft Bill, clause 28(6)(b).)

109. A manager should be entitled to be reimbursed for the reasonable expenses of discharging his or her functions. If the court so directs when appointing a manager, he or she shall be entitled to remuneration for discharging those functions. (Paragraphs 8.52 and draft Bill, clause 28(9).)

110. The Secretary of State should issue and from time to time revise a code of practice for the guidance of people who act as managers. (Paragraph 8.54 and draft Bill, clause 31(1)(c).)

PART IX – PUBLIC LAW PROTECTION FOR VULNERABLE PEOPLE AT RISK

111. A "vulnerable person" should mean any person of 16 or over who (1) is or may be in need of community care services by reason of mental or other disability, age or illness and who (2) is or may be unable to take care of himself or herself, or unable to protect himself or herself against significant harm or serious exploitation. (Paragraph 9.6 and draft Bill, clause 36(2).)

112. "Harm" should be defined to mean ill-treatment (including sexual abuse and forms of ill-treatment that are not physical); the impairment of, or an avoidable deterioration in, physical or mental health; and the impairment of physical, intellectual, emotional, social or behavioural development. (Paragraph 9.8 and draft Bill, clause 36(5).)

113. Where a local authority have reason to believe that a vulnerable person in their area is suffering or likely to suffer significant harm or serious exploitation they shall make such enquiries as they consider necessary to enable them to decide:

1) whether the person is in fact suffering or likely to suffer such harm or exploitation and

2) if so, whether community care services should be provided or arranged or other action taken to protect the person from such harm or exploitation. (Paragraph 9.16 and draft Bill, clause 37(1).)

114. Where an authorised officer of the local authority has reasonable cause to believe that a vulnerable person living in premises in the local authority's area is "at risk", the officer may at any reasonable time enter and inspect those premises and interview the person concerned in private. These powers should not be exercised if the offer knows or believes that the person concerned objects or would object unless the officer has reasonable cause to believe that the person concerned is or may be suffering from mental disability. (Paragraph 9.19 and draft Bill, clause 38(1) and (3).

115. On the application of an authorised officer, the court should have power to issue a warrant authorising a constable, accompanied by such an officer, to enter specified premises if:

1) the applicant has reasonable cause to believe that a vulnerable person living in those premises is "at risk";

2) granting the warrant is necessary to enable the officer to gain access to the vulnerable person, and

3) (unless there is reasonable cause to believe that the person is or may be suffering from mental disability) the applicant does not know or believe that the person objects or would object. (Paragraph 9.21 and draft Bill, clause 39.)

116. On the application of an authorised officer the court should have power to make an assessment order if:

1) the applicant has reasonable cause to believe that a vulnerable person is "at risk", and

2) the order is required so that the local authority can assess whether the person is in fact "at risk" and if so whether community care services should be provided or arranged, or other protective action taken, and

3) (unless there is reasonable cause to believe that the person is or may be suffering from mental disability) the applicant does not know or believe that the person objects or would object. (Paragraph 9.24 and draft Bill, clause 40(1) and (2).)

117. An assessment order should specify (1) the date by which the assessment is to begin, and (2) the period for which it will remain in force, being the shortest period necessary for the purposes of the assessment, not exceeding eight days. (Paragraph 9.25 and draft Bill, clause 40(4).)

118. Nothing to which the person concerned objects should be done pursuant to the assessment order unless the court has authorised it to be done notwithstanding that objection. (Paragraph 9.26 and draft Bill, clause 4)(3).)

119. A vulnerable person may only be removed from his or her place of residence pursuant to an assessment order in accordance with specific directions and for such period or periods as are specified in the order, and only if it is necessary for the purposes of the assessment. (Paragraph 9.27 and draft Bill, clause 40(5).)

120. On the application of an authorised officer, the court should have power to make a temporary protection order if:

1) a vulnerable person is likely to be "at risk" unless removed to or kept in protective accommodation for a short period, and

2) (unless there is reasonable cause to believe that the person is or may be suffering from mental disability) the applicant does not know or believe the person objects or would object to the order. (Paragraph 9.28 and draft Bill, clause 41(1) and (2).)

121. A temporary protection order should authorise removal to protective accommodation for a specified period being the shortest possible necessary for achieving the purpose of the order, with a maximum of eight days. (Paragraph 9.29 and draft Bill, clause 41(3).)

122. The court may, on the making of a temporary protection order, give directions for assessment as it may when making an assessment order. (Paragraph 9.31 and draft Bill, clause 41(4).)

123. Where a person has been removed to protective accommodation it shall be the duty of the local authority to return the person to the place from which he or she is removed as soon as that is practicable and consistent with his or her interests. (Paragraph 9.32 and draft Bill, clause 41(8).)

124. An application for a temporary protection order may be made ex parte. The person concerned, any donee of a CPA and any court-appointed manager should be entitled to apply for the discharge of an ex parte order. (Paragraph 9.33 and draft Bill, clause 41(5).)

125. It should be an offence for any person (other than the person concerned) without reasonable cause to obstruct (1) an authorised officer of a local authority in the exercise of his or her powers, or (2) any person who is acting pursuant to an assessment or temporary protection order. (Paragraph 9.36 and draft Bill, clause 42.)

126. Local authorities should have power to assist a vulnerable person in bringing proceedings for an order under the private law. (Paragraph 9.37 and draft Bill, clause 43.)

127. The existing duty to protect the movable property of a person removed from his or her place of residence should apply where a person is removed (1) pursuant to the local authority applying for an order under Part I of the Mental Incapacity Bill and (2) pursuant to an assessment or temporary protection order. (Paragraph 9.39 and draft Bill, clause 44.)

128. Local authorities should have power to take reasonable steps for the protection of the property and affairs of a person without capacity to protect them and for whom they provide or arrange accommodation. (Paragraph 9.40 and draft Bill, clause 35.)

129. Section 7(5) of the Mental Health Act 1983 should be amended so that only a local social services authority may be named as guardian. (Paragraph 9.49.)

130. Section 8(1) of the Mental Health Act 1983 should be amended to give a guardian an additional power to convey the patient to a residence specified by the guardian. (Paragraph 9.50.)

131. The powers of the Mental Health Act Commission should be extended to include those received into guardianship. (Paragraph 9.52.)

PART X – THE JUDICIAL FORUM

132. A new superior court of record called the Court of Protection should be established, and the office of the Supreme Court known as the Court of Protection should be abolished. (Paragraph 10.9 and draft Bill, clause 46(1).)

133. Magistrates' courts and single justices of the peace should have jurisdiction to deal with applications under Part II of the draft Bill only. (Paragraph 10.10 and draft Bill, clause 45(1)(b).)

134. Proceedings under Part II of the draft Bill should be treated as "family proceedings". (Paragraph 10.11 and draft Bill, clause 45(2).)

135. The jurisdiction of the Court of Protection should be exercised by judges nominated by the Lord Chancellor, whether Chancery Division or Family Division High Court judges, circuit judges or district judges. (Paragraph 10.13 and draft Bill, clause 46(2).)

136. The Lord Chancellor should designated one of the judges nominated as a Court of Protection judge to be Senior Judge of the Court of Protection. (Paragraph 10.14 and draft Bill, clause 46(4).)

137. The Lord Chancellor may appoint one of the judges of the High Court nominated as a Court of Protection judge to be President of the Court of Protection. (Paragraph 10.15 and draft Bill, clause 46(3).)

138. The Court of Protection should be able to sit at any place in England and Wales designated by the Lord Chancellor. (Paragraph 10.16 and draft Bill, clause 46(6).)

139. The Court of Protection should have a central office and registry in London. The Lord Chancellor should have power to designate additional registries outside London. (Paragraph 10.17 and draft Bill, clause 46(7).)

140. The Lord Chancellor should have power to provide by order for which kind of judge of the Court of Protection should deal with any particular proceedings and for the transfer of proceedings between the different kinds of judges. (Paragraph 10.18 and draft Bill, clause 46(5).)

141. The Lord Chancellor should have power to provide by order, in relation to persons who have not attained the age of eighteen, for the transfer of proceedings between a court having jurisdiction under the Mental Incapacity Act and a court having jurisdiction under the Children Act 1989. A court with either jurisdiction may decline to exercise it in respect of those under eighteen if the court considers that the issue can be more suitably dealt with by a court exercising the other jurisdiction. (Paragraph 10.19 and draft Bill, clause 45(3).)

142. Leave should be required before an application to the Court of Protection can be made. In granting leave the court should have regard to:

1) the applicant's connection with the person concerned,

2) the reasons for the application,

3) the benefit to the person concerned of any proposed order,

4) whether that benefit can be achieved in any other way.

No leave should be required for any application to the court by

1) a person who is alleged to be without capacity, or, in respect of such a person who is under 18 years old, any person with parental responsibility for that person,

2) a donee of a CPA granted by the person without capacity or a court-appointed manager,

3) the Public Trustee as respects any functions exercisable by virtue of an existing order, and

4) any person mentioned in an existing order of the court. (Paragraph 10.20 and draft Bill, clause 47.)

144. The Court of Protection should have power to make an order or give directions on a matter, pending a decision on whether the person concerned is without capacity in relation to that matter. (Paragraph 10.21 and draft Bill, clause 48.)

145. Appeals should lie:

    1) from a decision of a district judge to a circuit judge or a judge of the High Court;

    2) from a decision of a circuit judge or judge of the High Court given in the exercise of his or her original or appellate jurisdiction to the Court of Appeal. (Paragraph 10.22 and draft Bill, clause 49(1).)

146. Proceedings under the new jurisdiction should be conducted in accordance with rules made by the Lord Chancellor. (Paragraph 10.24 and draft Bill, clause 51.)

147. Where the person concerned is neither present nor represented, the court should (unless it considers it unnecessary) obtain a report on his or her wishes. (Paragraph 10.25 and draft Bill, clause 52(2).)

148. The Court of Protection should have power to ask a probation officer to report to the court, and power to ask a local authority officer to report or arrange for another person to report, on such matters as the court directs, relating to the person concerned. (Paragraph 10.26 and draft Bill, clause 52(1).)

149. It should be an offence to publish any material intended or likely to identify any person in respect of whom proceedings are brought under the new incapacity legislation. (Paragraph 10.28 and draft Bill, clause 54.)

annex

Glossary of Terms and Expressions

Advance Statement	An expression of views and preferences concerning medical treatment if the patient became incapacitated. An alternative term in common usage is 'living will'.
Advance Directive	Used by the Law Commission to refer to an advance decision about medical treatment the person wants to receive if they become incapacitated.
Advance Refusal	The individual's refusal of some or all types of medical treatment which might be administered if they become incapacitated.

NB: Advance statements, advance directives, and advance refusals must be made when the patient has the capacity to form the relevant views or take the relevant decisions.

Amicus Curiae	[Latin: friend of the court] Counsel who assists the court by putting arguments in support of an interest that might not be adequately represented by the parties to the proceedings (such as the public interest) or by arguing on behalf of a party who is otherwise unrepresented.
Attorney	See *power of attorney*.
Continuing Power of Attorney	The Law Commission have proposed the creation of a Continuing Power of Attorney, which would integrate a reformed scheme of enduring powers of attorney into a unified scheme which provides for other substitute decision-making procedures. See Chapter 6 of this Green Paper.
Court of Protection	The Court is an office of the Supreme Court. It exists to protect the property and affairs of persons who, through mental disorder, are incapable of managing their own financial affairs. The Court's powers are wide ranging but are limited to dealing with the

financial and legal affairs of the person concerned. Proposals for reform of the role of the Court of Protection are considered in Chapter 9 of this paper.

Enduring Power of Attorney

An Enduring Power of Attorney is a power of attorney which, subject to conditions and safeguards, continues in force even after the maker of the Enduring Power (the 'Donor') becomes mentally incapable of handling his or her affairs, provided that it is registered. It can be used by the Attorney from the date of its execution and prior to the onset of mental incapacity, provided that there are no restrictions placed within the document and if this is what the Donor wishes. The purpose of an Enduring Power of Attorney is to enable people, while they are still mentally capable, to decide who they would like to deal with their financial affairs for them after they become mentally incapable. The Enduring Power of Attorney was introduced by the Enduring Powers of Attorney Act 1985.

Euthanasia

A deliberate intervention undertaken with the express intention of ending a life, albeit at the person's own request or for a merciful motive.

Guardian ad Litem

In the context of mental incapacity, a person appointed by the court to protect the interests of a person under disability, who may not otherwise acknowledge service, defend, make a counterclaim or intervene in any proceedings, or appear in any proceedings under a judgement or order notice of which has been served on him.

Health Care Team

The doctors, nurses and other professionals involved in the care and medical treatment of the individual patient.

Living Will

See *advance statement*.

Lord Chancellor's Visitors

There are three types of visitor: medical visitors, legal visitors and general visitors. Medical visitors, whose role is of relevance to mental incapacity, are "registered medical practitioners who appear to the Lord Chancellor to have special knowledge and experience of cases of mental disorder" (Section 102 (3) (a) of the Mental Health Act 1983). The are currently six such visitors, each of whom deals with visits in a specified area of the country.

Official Solicitor

The Official Solicitor is an officer of the Supreme Court, whose duties have as their purpose: (a) the prevention of a possible denial of justice to any individual or party to proceedings; (b) safeguarding the welfare, property and status of persons under legal disability or at disadvantage before the law; and (c) the facilitation of the administration of justice (as investigator, confidential adviser to judges and others, or by the instruction of counsel as *amicus curiae*).

Palliative Care   For a patient who is terminally ill, palliative care may be the most appropriate course which the health-care team can offer. The World Health Organisation has described palliative care as "a form of care that recognises that cure or long-term control is not possible; is concerned with the quality rather than quantity of life; and cloaks troublesome and distressing symptoms with treatments whose primary or sole aim is the highest possible measure of patient comfort". The Department of Health said "palliative care is active total care provided to a patient when it is recognised that the illness is no longer curable. Palliative care concentrates on the quality of life and on alleviating pain and other distressing symptoms, and is intended neither to hasten nor postpone death".

Power of Attorney   A power of attorney is a means whereby one person (the donor) gives legal authority to another person (the attorney or donee) to manage the donor's affairs. See also *Enduring Power of Attorney* and *Continuing Power of Attorney*.

Public Trust Office   An Executive Agency within the Lord Chancellor's Department. Among other duties, responsible for the day to day administration of cases under the jurisdiction of the *Court of Protection*. Also responsible for the registration of *Enduring Powers of Attorney*.

Background Information on the Court of Protection, the Public Trust Office, and the Official Solicitor

THE COURT OF PROTECTION

The Court of Protection (the Court) is an Office of the Supreme Court. Its function is to manage and administer the property and affairs of people who through reason of mental disorder are incapable of managing their own affairs. The Court draws its powers from the Mental Health Act 1983, the Enduring Powers of Attorney Act 1985, the Court of Protection Rules 1994 and the Court of Protection (Enduring Powers of Attorney) Rules 1994.

THE PUBLIC TRUST OFFICE

The Public Trust Office came into being on the 2 January 1987; it was formed from a number of different organisations which dealt with the management of the financial affairs of private individuals. The Mental Health Sector is divided into the operational areas of the Protection Division and the Receivership Division. The Protection Division provides administrative services to the Court, deals with the registration of Enduring Powers of Attorney and manages patients' financial affairs in conjunction with a Receiver appointed by the Court. The Receivership Division's purpose is to act as Receiver where no one else is willing or able to act or where the Court decides to appoint the Public Trustee as an independent party to act as Receiver, and is responsible for all of a patient's day to day requirements. On 1 July 1994 the Public Trust Office became an Executive Agency within the Lord Chancellor's Department.

Numbers of Enduring Powers of Attorney

The following table shows the numbers of applications for registration of an EPA received in each year since 1986:

1986	605	**1992**	5189
1987	1476	**1993**	5767
1988	2215	**1994**	6637
1989	2842	**1995**	7562
1990	3549	**1996**	8921
1991	4306	**To 1 Oct 1997**	7186

The following table shows the number of registrations for EPA made each year since 1992:

1992	3374	**1995**	5642
1993	3826	**1996**	6630
1994	4603	**1997**	5840

THE OFFICIAL SOLICITOR

A central element of the Official Solicitor's duties is safeguarding the welfare, property and status of persons under a legal disability or at a disadvantage before the law. He deals with some 950 new cases of proceedings involving adults under mental incapacity each year. Many of these relate to a wide spread of litigation of all categories, mainly affecting financial rights or liabilities, from possession actions in the county courts to heavy personal injuries litigation in the High Court, but two increasingly important areas of work are declaratory proceedings in the High Court and medical treatment decisions. The former include cases where the issues centre on where a person under disability is to live and with whom he or she is to have contact. The latter require him to act as guardian ad litem or amicus curiae in respect of treatment such as sterilisation, abortion, emergency caesareans and end-of-life decisions such as the withdrawal of nutrition and hydration from a patient in PVS.

It is the aim of the Official Solicitor:

1) by his intervention in proceedings in a representational role or otherwise;

2) in the absence of any other appropriate person or agency; and

3) in as economical, effective and expeditious manner as practicable;

to perform duties which have as their purpose –

a) the prevention of a possible denial of justice to any individual or party to proceedings (including safeguarding the liberty of the subject);

b) safeguarding the welfare, property and status of persons under legal disability or at a disadvantage before the law;

c) the facilitation of the administration of justice (as investigator, confidential adviser to judges and others or by the instruction of counsel as amicus curiae).

To achieve that aim the Official Solicitor must:

decide promptly upon invitations to be appointed to represent persons under a legal disability, and to safeguard and advance their interests by effective and efficient representation when appointed;

act economically and efficiently as trustee or administrator, and to invest funds securely to provide the optimum return on capital and provision of income, as appropriate;

support the judges by giving them timely and effective advice and assistance when called upon to do so; and

train and motivate staff to enable these activities to be done effectively.

Printed in the UK for The Stationery Office Limited on behalf of the
Controller of Her Majesty's Stationery Office
Dd 5067818   12/97   76368   Job No 34028